Garden-Fresh
Cross-Stitch™

Edited by Vicki Blizzard

the Needlecraft® Shop

Garden-Fresh Cross-Stitch

Copyright © 2006 The Needlecraft Shop, Berne, Indiana 46711

Editor: Vicki Blizzard
Managing Editor: Barb Sprunger
Technical Editor: Marla Freeman
Copy Editor: Michelle Beck

Photography Supervisor: Tammy Christian
Photographers: Don Clark, Christena Green, Matthew Owen
Photography Stylists: Tammy Nussbaum, Tammy M. Smith
Production Coordinator: Erin Augsburger
Graphic Arts Supervisor: Ronda Bechinski
Art Director: Brad Snow
Assistant Art Director: Nick Pierce
Graphic Artist: Pam Gregory
Production Assistants: Cheryl Kempf, Marj Morgan
Technical Artists: Marla Freeman, Judy Neuenschwander
Publishing Services Manager: Brenda Gallmeyer

Chief Executive Officer: John Robinson
Publishing Director: David J. McKee
Marketing Director: Dan Fink

© 2006

TOLL-FREE ORDER LINE or to request a free catalog (800) 582-6643
Customer Service (800) 282-6643, **Fax** (800) 882-6643
Visit www.AnniesAttic.com

ISBN: 1-57367-236-X   Library of Congress Number: 2005908423

Printed in USA   1 2 3 4 5 6 7 8 9

Garden-Fresh Cross-Stitch

Introduction

I love working in my garden beds. Every winter, I yearn for the day I can plant seeds in flats and watch them sprout. I baby those seedlings until the proper planting time, and then I carefully nurture them in their outside beds until they grow into mature flower and vegetable plants. Garden time is "me" time, although I readily share the fruits of my labor with family and friends.

If you also enjoy gardens—even if that enjoyment is just watching a neighbor's lilac bush bloom in the spring—you'll love the projects in this book. Each of them beautifully illustrates a garden theme, such as the azaleas blooming in a wooded clearing by a lake or fresh produce from a farmer's market.

I'll be taking my cross-stitch projects outside so that I can stitch while I watch my garden grow. Won't you join me in spirit?

Warm regards,

Vicki Blizzard

Contents

Watering Cans

Design by Mike Vickery

These delightfully decorated watering cans will add a special touch to a gardner's abode. Hung in an entryway, this piece extends a warm welcome to all who visit.

Materials
- Jonquil yellow 14-count Aida:
  12 x 20-inches
- Shaker peg rack 22x13 inches

"Watering Cans" was stitched on jonquil yellow 14-count Aida from Wichelt using DMC floss. Shaker Peg Rack #10101 from Sudberry House.

Skill Level
**Average

Stitch Count
199 wide x 72 high

Approximate Design Size
11-count 18⅛" x 6⅝"
14-count 14¼" x 5¼"
16-count 12½" x 4½"
18-count 11⅛" x 4"
22-count 9⅛" x 3⅜"

Instructions
1. Center and stitch design, using three strands floss for Cross-Stitch and one strand floss for Backstitch. ❖

CROSS-STITCH (3X)

ANCHOR		DMC	COLORS
2	·	White	White
109	♠	209	Dark lavender
108	=	210	Medium lavender
342	□	211	Light lavender
118	‡	340	Medium blue violet
117	⊙	341	Light blue violet
9			352	Light coral
8	⫷	353	Peach
261	▷	368	Light pistachio green
1043	+	369	Very light pistachio green
398	⌇	415	Pearl gray
1045	✕	436	Tan
362	::	437	Light tan

CROSS-STITCH (3X)

ANCHOR		DMC	COLORS
96	⌀	554	Light violet
293	⊞	727	Very light topaz
234	◊	762	Very light pearl gray
128	/	775	Very light baby blue
24	Ħ	776	Medium pink
23	∧	818	Baby pink
390	✿	822	Light beige gray
52	↘	899	Medium rose
204	๑	913	Medium Nile green
850	⅄	926	Medium gray green
848	∴	927	Light gray green
274	−	928	Very light gray green
203	◈	954	Nile green

CROSS-STITCH (3X)

ANCHOR		DMC	COLORS
206	✳	955	Light Nile green
887	◇	3046	Medium yellow beige
852	⊞	3047	Light yellow beige
129	◤	3325	Light baby blue
120	~	3747	Very light blue violet
140	☆	3755	Baby blue
216	⌗	3815	Dark celadon green
215	▥	3816	Celadon green
213	✳	3817	Light celadon green
275	○	3823	Ultra pale yellow

BACKSTITCH (1X)

ANCHOR		DMC	COLOR
236	▬	3799	Very dark pewter gray

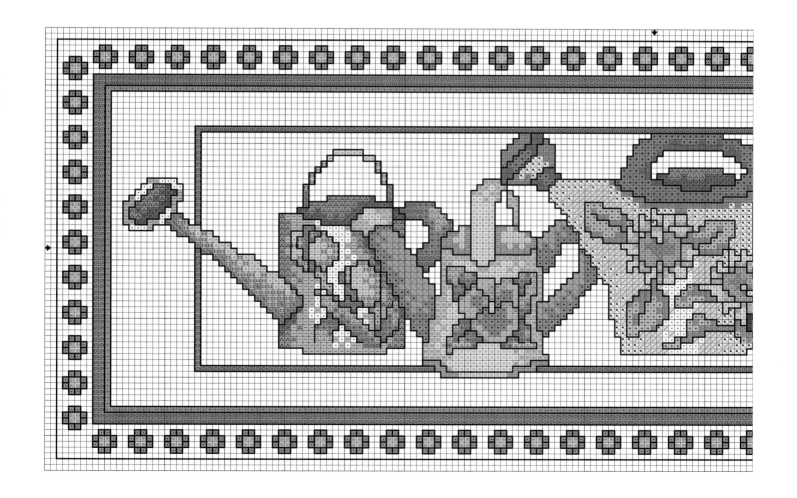

CROSS-STITCH (3X)

ANCHOR	DMC	COLORS
2	White	White
109	209	Dark lavender
108	210	Medium lavender
342	211	Light lavender
118	340	Medium blue violet
117	341	Light blue violet
9	352	Light coral
8	353	Peach
261	368	Light pistachio green
1043	369	Very light pistachio green
398	415	Pearl gray
1045	436	Tan
362	437	Light tan

CROSS-STITCH (3X)

ANCHOR	DMC	COLORS
96	554	Light violet
293	727	Very light topaz
234	762	Very light pearl gray
128	775	Very light baby blue
24	776	Medium pink
23	818	Baby pink
390	822	Light beige gray
52	899	Medium rose
204	913	Medium Nile green
850	926	Medium gray green
848	927	Light gray green
274	928	Very light gray green
203	954	Nile green

CROSS-STITCH (3X)

ANCHOR	DMC	COLORS
206	955	Light Nile green
887	3046	Medium yellow beige
852	3047	Light yellow beige
129	3325	Light baby blue
120	3747	Very light blue violet
140	3755	Baby blue
216	3815	Dark celadon green
215	3816	Celadon green
213	3817	Light celadon green
275	3823	Ultra pale yellow

BACKSTITCH (1X)

ANCHOR	DMC	COLOR
236	3799	Very dark pewter gray

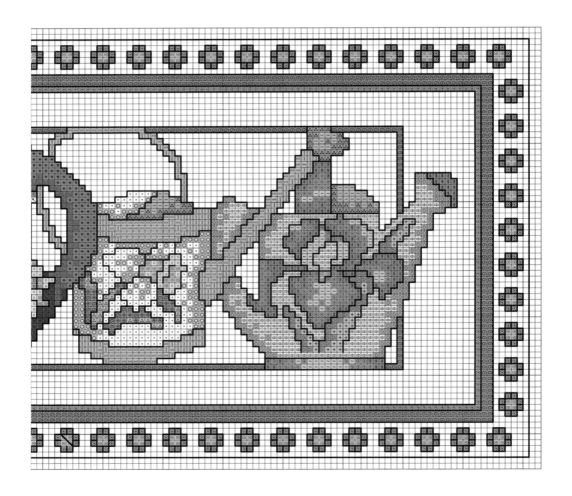

Butterflies Are Free

Design by True Colors

Cheery butterflies and fairies provide whimsical decor for a young girl's room. Chances are she won't want to give them up when she gets older!

Materials
• Blue hand-dyed 28-count evenweave fabric:
    20 x 15 inches

"Butterflies Are Free" was stitched on blue hand-dyed 28-count evenweave fabric using DMC floss. Finished piece was custom framed.

Skill Level
**Average

Stitch Count
176 wide x 93 high

Approximate Design Size
11-count 16" x 8½"
14-count 12½" x 6⅝"
16-count 11" x 5⅞"
18-count 9¾" x 5⅛"

22-count 8" x 4¼"
28-count over two threads 12½" x 6⅝"

Instructions
1. Center and stitch design on evenweave fabric, stitching over two threads and using three strands floss for Cross-Stitch, and one strand floss for Backstitch. ❖

CROSS-STITCH (3X)

ANCHOR		DMC	COLORS
2	·	White	White
38	◆	335	Rose
98	▣	553	Violet
228	✦	700	Bright green
301	⁞⁞	744	Pale yellow
275	▢	746	Off white
1022	♡	760	Salmon

CROSS-STITCH (3X)

ANCHOR		DMC	COLORS
307	╱	783	Medium topaz
131	✳	798	Dark Delft blue
144	+	800	Pale Delft blue
130	▢	809	Delft blue
52	⌘	899	Medium rose
209			912	Light emerald green
204	∿	913	Medium Nile green

CROSS-STITCH (3X)

ANCHOR		DMC	COLORS
101	~	1948	Very light peach
868	○	3779	Ultra very light terra cotta
236	◉	3799	Very dark pewter gray
111	◤	3837	Ultra dark lavender

BACKSTITCH (1X)

ANCHOR		DMC	COLORS
936	━	632	Ultra very dark desert sand
923	━	699	Green
309	━	781	Very dark topaz
133	━	796	Dark royal blue
45	━	814	Dark garnet
236	━	3799	Very dark pewter gray*
111	━	3837	Ultra dark lavender*

Duplicate color

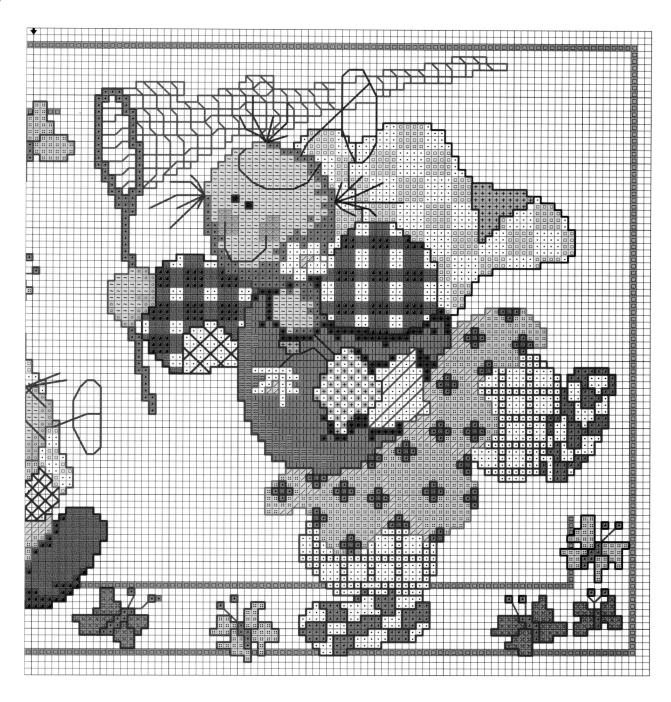

Bright Butterflies

Design by True Colors

These cheerful butterflies resting on sunshine-yellow daisies make wonderful companions to Butterflies Are Free on page 9.

Materials
• Blue hand-dyed 28-count evenweave fabric: 2 (11 x 13-inch) pieces

"Butterflies Are Free" was stitched on blue hand-dyed 28-count evenweave fabric using DMC floss. Finished piece was custom framed.

Skill Level
**Average

Stitch Count
63 wide x 93 high

Approximate Design Size
11-count 5¾" x 8½"
14-count 4½" x 6⅝"
16-count 4" x 5⅞"
18-count 3½" x 5⅛"
22-count 2⅞" x 4¼"
28-count over two threads 4½" x 6⅝"

Instructions
1. Center and stitch design on evenweave fabric, stitching over two threads and using three strands floss for Cross-Stitch, two strands floss for French Knot and one strand floss for Backstitch. ❖

CROSS-STITCH (2X)

ANCHOR		DMC	COLORS
38	✚	335	Rose
98	⊘	553	Violet
46	▮	666	Bright red
228	~	700	Bright green
305	ℐ	725	Medium light topaz
301	‖	744	Pale yellow
307	✳	783	Medium topaz
142	✚	798	Dark delft blue
144	◖	800	Pale delft blue
130	−	809	Delft blue
52	◨	899	Medium rose
209	⧅	912	Light emerald green
204	◗	913	Medium Nile green
236	◉	3799	Very dark pewter gray
111	▥	3837	Ultra dark lavender

BACKSTITCH (1X)

ANCHOR		DMC	COLORS
936	—	632	Ultra very dark desert sand
923	—	699	Green
309	—	781	Very dark topaz
133	—	796	Dark royal blue
45	—	814	Dark garnet
236	—	3799	Very dark pewter gray*

FRENCH KNOT (2X)

ANCHOR		DMC	COLOR
236	●	3799	Very dark pewter gray*

*Duplicate color

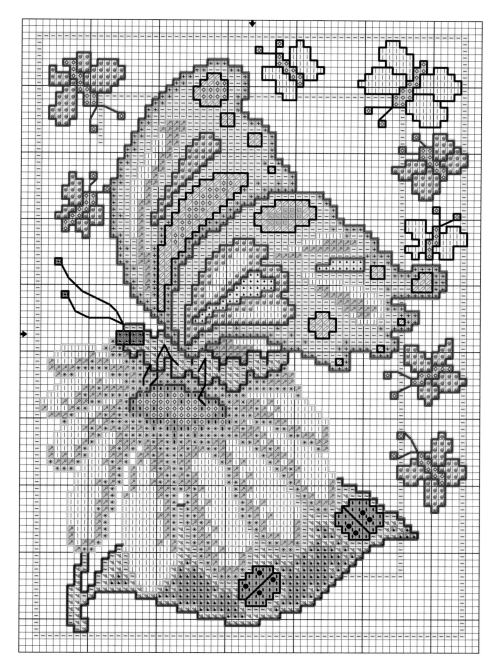

CROSS-STITCH (2X)

ANCHOR	DMC	COLORS
38	335	Rose
98	553	Violet
46	666	Bright red
228	700	Bright green
305	725	Medium light topaz
301	744	Pale yellow
307	783	Medium topaz
142	798	Dark delft blue
144	800	Pale delft blue
130	809	Delft blue
52	899	Medium rose
209	912	Light emerald green
204	913	Medium Nile green
236	3799	Very dark pewter gray
111	3837	Ultra dark lavender

BACKSTITCH (1X)

ANCHOR	DMC	COLORS
936	632	Ultra very dark desert sand
923	699	Green
309	781	Very dark topaz
133	796	Dark royal blue
45	814	Dark garnet
236	3799	Very dark pewter gray*

FRENCH KNOT (2X)

ANCHOR	DMC	COLOR
236	3799	Very dark pewter gray*

*Duplicate color

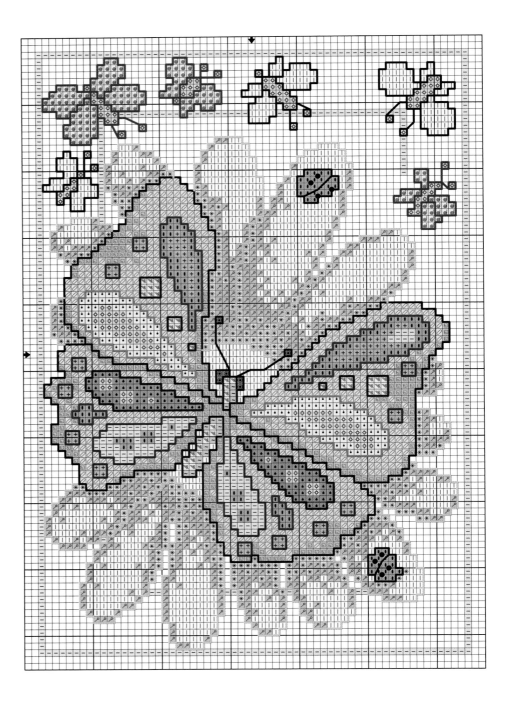

Dragonflies

Design by Mike Vickery

*Gossamer-winged dragonflies reflect the
wonder of nature's glory and lend a fresh
summer feel to your decor.*

Materials:
- Delicate teal 28-count Jobelan: 12 x 18 inches
- Three 7 x 7-inch pieces of 14-count perforated paper
- Three bamboo skewers
- Craft glue or glue gun

"Dragonflies" was stitched on Jobelan by Wichelt Imports Inc., using DMC floss. Finished piece was custom framed.

Skill Level
***Challenging

Stitch Count
176 wide x 88 high

Approximate Design Size
11-count 16" x 8"
14-count 12⅝" x 6⅜"
16-count 11" x 5½"
18-count 9⅞" x 5"
22-count 8" x 4"
28-count over two threads 12⅝" x 6⅜"

Instructions
1. For framed piece, center and stitch design onto Jobelan, using two strands floss for Cross-Stitch and one strand floss for Backstitch.

2. For Plant Pokes, center and stitch one dragonfly motif onto each piece of perforated paper using two strands floss for Cross-Stitch and one strand floss for Backstitch.

Finishing
1. Carefully trim each Plant Poke design following outline of design. Glue one design to each skewer as shown in photo. ❖

CROSS-STITCH (2X)

ANCHOR		DMC	COLORS
403	♠	310	Black
978	✖	322	Dark dark baby blue
119	➜	333	Very dark blue violet
118	m	340	Medium blue violet
117	‹	341	Light blue violet
401	◈	413	Dark pewter gray
305	Y	725	Medium light topaz
293	L	727	Very light topaz
310	▲	780	Ultra very dark topaz
308	≪	782	Dark topaz
307	δ	783	Medium topaz

CROSS-STITCH (2X)

ANCHOR		DMC	COLORS
390	+	822	Light beige gray
205	✕	911	Medium emerald green
204	3	913	Medium Nile green
187	$	958	Dark seagreen
185	L	964	Light seagreen
887	✳	3046	Medium yellow beige
852	U	3047	Light yellow beige
68	◀	3687	Mauve
66	=	3688	Medium mauve
49	)	3689	Light mauve
1030	⌘	3746	Dark blue violet

CROSS-STITCH (2X)

ANCHOR		DMC	COLORS
120	✎	3747	Very light blue violet
140	I	3755	Baby blue
69	▼	3803	Dark mauve
275	/	3823	Ultra pale yellow
2	·	White	White

BACKSTITCH (1X)

ANCHOR		DMC	COLORS
236	—	3799	Very dark pewter gray

Garden Buddies

Designs by Ursula Michael

Gentle garden creatures alight inside these acrylic coasters—they're a year-round reminder of a beautiful summer.

Materials
- White 14-count Aida:
  4 (7 x 7-inch) pieces
- 4 square acrylic coasters with 3-inch openings for needlework

"Garden Buddies" coasters were stitched on white 14-count Aida by Zweigart using DMC floss.

Skill Level
**Average

Coaster Stitch Count
34 wide x 34 high

Approximate Design Size
11-count 3" x 3"
14-count 2⅜" x 2⅜"
16-count 2" x 2"
18-count 1⅞" x 1⅞"
22-count 1½" x 1½"

Instructions
1. Center and stitch design, using three strands floss for Cross-Stitch and one strand floss for Backstitch.

Finishing
1. Insert in acrylic coaster form following manufacturer's instructions. ❖

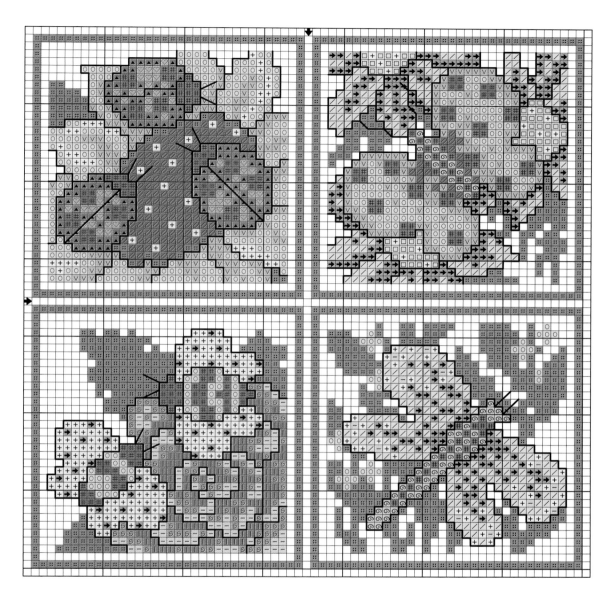

CROSS-STITCH (3X)

ANCHOR		DMC	COLORS
109	◻	209	Dark lavender
42	▯	309	Dark rose
9046	▲	321	Red
926	+	712	Cream
295	○	726	Light topaz
304	V	741	Medium tangerine
24	−	776	Medium pink
161	➜	813	Light blue
158	╱	828	Ultra very light blue
52	6	899	Medium rose

CROSS-STITCH (3X)

ANCHOR		DMC	COLORS
1004	╱	920	Medium copper
243	∷	988	Medium forest green
905	#	3021	Very dark brown gray
831	௭	3782	Light mocha brown
35	♡	3801	Very dark melon

BACKSTITCH (1X)

ANCHOR		DMC	COLOR
905	—	3021	Very dark brown gray*

Duplicate color

Bumblebee Fancy

Design by Mike Vickery

Add a little sparkle to your stitching with this amusing chubby bumblebee!

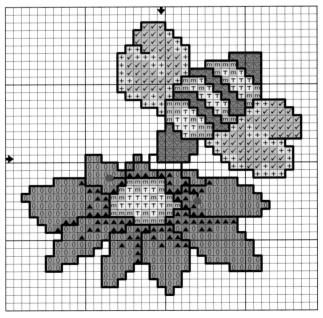

Materials

- Opalescent 14-count Aida: 7 x 7 inches
- 4-inch diameter basket with pincushion insert
- 15-inch length of gimp braid
- Craft glue or glue gun

"Bumblebee Fancy" was stitched on opalescent 14-count Aida by Zweigart using DMC floss and Kreinik #8 Fine Braid. Small Nantucket Lightship Basket #30000 with Pincushion Insert #30001 shown is by Sudberry House.

Skill Level

**Average

Stitch Count

35 wide x 35 high

Approximate Design Size

11-count 3¼" x 3¼"
14-count 2½" x 2½"
16-count 2¼" x 2¼"
18-count 2" x 2"
22-count 1⅝" x 1⅝"

Instructions

1. Center and stitch design using two strands floss or one strand fine braid for Cross-Stitch, and one strand floss for Backstitch and French Knot.

Finishing

1. Position and mount design on pincushion insert following manufacturer's instructions; glue gimp braid around design as shown in photo. ❖

CROSS-STITCH (2X)

ANCHOR		DMC	COLORS
401	♡	413	Dark pewter gray
305	m	725	Medium light topaz
293	T	727	Very light topaz
131	▲	798	Dark delft blue
136	0	799	Medium delft blue
2	✓	White	White

CROSS-STITCH (1X)

KREINIK #8 FINE BRAID

032	+	Pearl

BACKSTITCH (1X)

ANCHOR		DMC	COLOR
236	—	3799	Very dark pewter gray

FRENCH KNOT (1X)

ANCHOR		DMC	COLOR
236	●	3799	Very dark pewter gray*

*Duplicate color

Classic Flowers

Design by Mike Vickery

Celebrate the joy of spring flowers all year long with this timeless beauty.

Materials

- White 28-count Meran:
  13 x 21 inches
- 20cm bell pull

"Classic Flowers" was stitched on Meran by Zweigart, using DMC floss. Bell pull shown is by Wichelt Imports Inc.

Skill Level
**Average

Stitch Count
95 wide x 210 high

Approximate Design Size
11-count 8⅝" x 19⅛"
14-count 6⅞" x 15"
16-count 6" x 13⅛"
18-count 5⅜" x 11¾"
22-count 4⅜" x 9⅝"
28-count over two threads 6⅞" x 15"

Instructions
1. Center and stitch design, stitching over two threads and using two strands floss for Cross-Stitch and one strand floss for Backstitch.

Finishing
1. Trim design to 15 x 19 inches.

2. Using a ½-inch seam allowance, sew long edges together, right sides facing, to form a tube. Turn right side out; press with seam in center back.

3. Fold under a 1-inch hem on top and

bottom edges; slip stitch in place. Insert bell pull into folded edges following manufacturer's instructions. ❖

CROSS-STITCH (2X)

ANCHOR		DMC	COLORS
110	❖	208	Very dark lavender
342	c	211	Light lavender
830	⊠	644	Medium beige gray
228	✿	700	Bright green
226	♥	702	Kelly green
256	✛	704	Bright chartreuse

CROSS-STITCH (2X)

ANCHOR		DMC	COLORS
305	$	725	Topaz
293	↓	727	Very light topaz
259	4	772	Very light yellow green
128	~	775	Very light baby blue
24	0	776	Medium pink
307	‡	783	Medium topaz
23	<	818	Baby pink
390	6	822	Light beige gray
218	◉	890	Ultra dark pistachio green
52	▲	899	Medium rose
229	T	910	Dark emerald green
209	⊡	912	Light emerald green
203	φ	954	Nile green
129	★	3325	Light baby blue
266	◢	3347	Medium yellow green
264	◆	3348	Light yellow green
87	✿	3607	Light plum
85	◊	3609	Ultra light plum
236	⌐	3823	Ultra pale yellow
2	–	White	White

BACKSTITCH (1X)

ANCHOR		DMC	COLOR
236	—	3799	Very dark pewter gray*

*Duplicate color

Mexican Talavera Tile

Design by Barbara Sestok

In Mexico, ceramic tiles in this style decorate cupolas, facades of monasteries and buildings, and are the quintessential element of baroque architecture in the city of Puebla.

Materials

- Antique white sham for 10 x 10-inch pillow form with 14-count Aida front panel
- Polyester fiberfill or 10-inch-square pillow form

"Mexican Talavera Tile" was stitched on antique white 14-count Lady Elizabeth pillow sham #PS-7780-0322 from Charles Craft Inc., using Anchor floss.

Skill Level

*Easy

Stitch Count

45 wide x 45 high

Approximate Design Size

11-count 4" x 4"
14-count 3¼" x 3¼"
16-count 2⅞" x 2⅞"
18-count 2½" x 2½"
22-count 2" x 2"

Instructions

1. Center and stitch design on sham, stitching over one thread and using three strands floss for Cross-Stitch and two strands floss for Backstitch.

Finishing

1. Insert fiberfill or pillow form in sham. ❖

CROSS-STITCH (3X)

DMC		ANCHOR	COLORS
White	·	2	White
803		148	Ultra very dark baby blue
3325	~	129	Light baby blue
3760	⌘	161	Medium wedgewood
319	∧	218	Very dark pistachio green
702	✿	226	Kelly green
745	⌄	300	Light pale yellow
721	⊕	324	Medium orange spice

BACKSTITCH (2X)

DMC		ANCHOR	COLORS
803	—	148	Ultra very dark baby blue*
319	—	218	Very dark pistachio green*
920	—	340	Medium copper

*Duplicate color

Chapeau Rouge

Design by Pamela Kellogg

Fine gold braid and seed beads add sparkle and shine to a gorgeous hat with a sassy attitude!

Materials
- Angel blush 28-count Lugana: 18 x 12½ inches
- Kreinik blending filament: star mauve #093
- Kreinik #4 very fine braid: gold #002HL
- Mill Hill glass seed beads: crystal honey #02019

"Chapeau Rouge" was stitched on angel blush 28-count Lugana from Zweigart with DMC floss, Kreinik blending filament and #4 very fine braid and Mill Hill glass seed beads. Finished piece was custom framed.

Skill Level
**Average

Stitch Count
170 wide x 93 high

Approximate Design Size
11-count 15½" x 8½"
14-count 12⅛" x 6⅝"
16-count 10⅝" x 5⅞"
18-count 9½" x 5⅛"
22-count 7¾" x 4¼"
28-count over two threads 12⅛" x 6⅝"

Instructions
1. Center and stitch design on 28-count Lugana, stitching over two threads using three strands floss, or two strands floss and one strand blending filament for Cross-Stitch. Use two strands white floss for Backstitch on feathers, and one strand floss or very fine braid for remaining Backstitch.

2. Attach beads (see Bead Attachment illustration on page 136) as indicated on graph using one strand light straw floss. ❖

CROSS-STITCH (3X)

ANCHOR		DMC	COLORS	
2	·	White	White	
109	♣	209	Dark lavender	
108	∷	210	Medium lavender	
342	–	211	Light lavender	
1006	△	304	Medium red	
9046	=	321	Red	
1005	*	498	Dark red	
99	▣	552	Medium violet	
98	/	553	Violet	
46	Y	666	Bright red	

CROSS-STITCH (3X)

ANCHOR		DMC	COLORS
259	≡	772	Very light yellow green
24	·ı·	776	Medium pink
23	✕	818	Baby pink
271	⊿	819	Light baby pink
1044	●	895	Very dark hunter green
268	♡	3345	Dark hunter green
267	▲	3346	Hunter green
266	♪	3347	Medium yellow green
264	❂	3348	Light yellow green
33	◇	3706	Medium melon

CROSS-STITCH (3X)

ANCHOR		DMC	COLORS
31	~	3708	Light melon
35	◊	3801	Very dark melon
295	⅍	3822	Light straw

KREINIK BLENDED CROSS-STITCH

ANCHOR		DMC	COLORS
118	⊥	340	Medium blue violet (2X) with 093 star mauve BF (1X)
117	⋒	341	Light blue violet (2X) with 093 star mauve BF (1X)

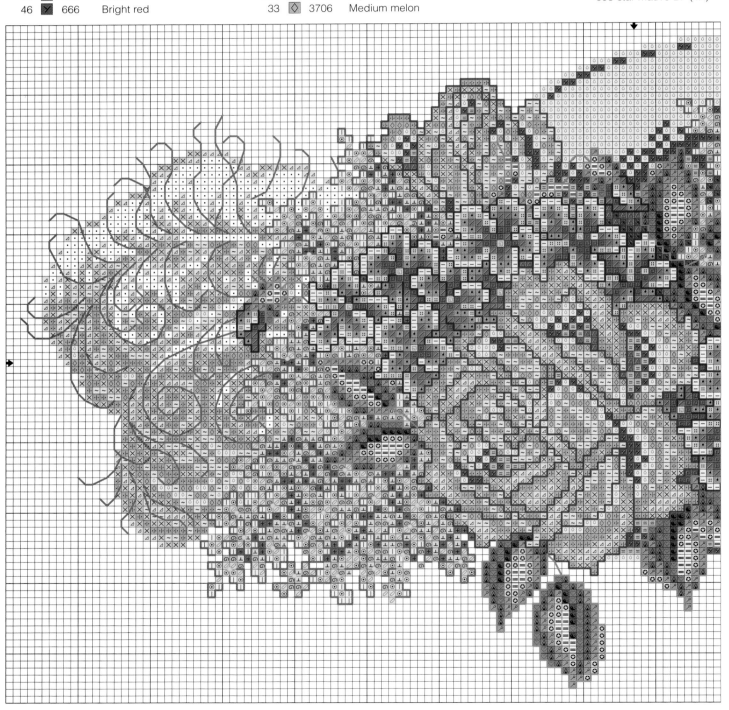

KREINIK BLENDED CROSS-STITCH

ANCHOR		DMC	COLORS
128	◉	775	Very light baby blue (2X) with 093 star mauve BF (1X)
1030	➕	3746	Dark blue violet (2X) with 093 star mauve BF (1X)
120	⊘	3747	Very light blue violet (2X) with 093 star mauve BF (1X)
1037	⊡	3756	Ultra very light baby blue (2X) with 093 star mauve BF (1X)

BACKSTITCH (2X)

ANCHOR	DMC	COLOR
2	▬ White	White (feathers)

BACKSTITCH (1X)

ANCHOR		DMC	COLORS
1006	▬	304	Medium red* (rose, rosebud)
119	▬	333	Very dark blue violet (lilacs)
102	▬	550	Very dark violet (violets)
1044	▬	895	Very dark hunter green* leaves, stems)

KREINIK #4 BRAID   COLOR

002HL	▬	Gold (hatband)

ATTACH BEAD

MILL HILL SEED BEAD

02019	○	Crystal honey, with 3822 light straw (1X)

Duplicate color

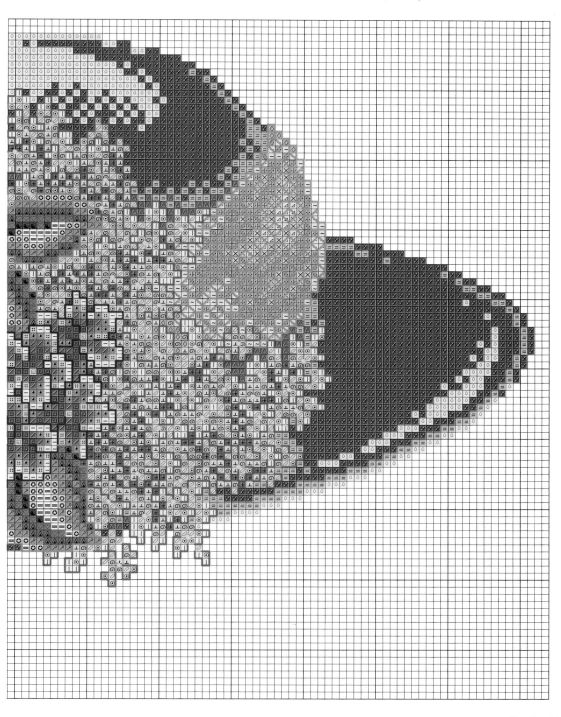

With All My Heart

Design by Pamela Kellogg

A handsome bluebird presents his lady with a beautiful rose in this celebration of springtime love.

Materials
- Ivory 28-count Jobelan:
  18 x 19 inches

"With All My Heart" was stitched on ivory 28-count Jobelan by Wichelt using DMC floss. Finished piece was custom framed.

Skill Level
**Average

Stitch Count
145 wide x 159 high

Approximate Design Size
11-count 13⅛" x 14½"
14-count 10⅜" x 11⅜"
16-count 9" x 10"
18-count 8" x 8⅞"
22-count 6½" x 7¼"

28-count over two threads
10⅜" x 11⅜"

Instructions
1. Center and stitch design, stitching over two threads and using three strands floss for Cross-Stitch and one strand floss for Backstitch. Use two strands floss for French Knot, wrapping needle twice. ❖

CROSS-STITCH (3X)

ANCHOR		DMC	COLORS
59		150	Ultra very dark dusty rose
48		151	Very light dusty rose
175		157	Very light cornflower blue
403		310	Black
400		317	Pewter gray
218		319	Very dark pistachio green
215		320	Medium pistachio green
217		367	Dark pistachio green
214		368	Light pistachio green
1043		369	Very light pistachio green
401		413	Dark pewter gray
235		414	Dark steel gray
358		433	Medium brown
310		434	Light brown
1046		435	Very light brown
1045		436	Tan
267		469	Avocado green
266		470	Light avocado green
265		471	Very light avocado green
253		472	Ultra light avocado green
162		517	Dark wedgewood
1039		518	Light wedgewood
1038		519	Sky blue
275		746	Off white
158		747	Very light sky blue (2 skeins)
259		772	Very light yellow green

CROSS-STITCH (3X)

ANCHOR		DMC	COLORS
308		782	Dark topaz
307		783	Medium topaz
178		791	Very dark cornflower blue
941		792	Dark cornflower blue
176		793	Medium cornflower blue
175		794	Light cornflower blue
359		801	Dark coffee brown
218		890	Ultra dark pistachio green
1044		895	Very dark hunter green
360		898	Very dark coffee brown
861		935	Dark avocado green
269		936	Very dark avocado green
268		937	Medium avocado green
292		3078	Very light golden yellow
268		3345	Dark hunter green
267		3346	Hunter green
266		3347	Medium yellow green
264		3348	Light yellow green
59		3350	Ultra dark dusty rose
74		3354	Light dusty rose
76		3731	Very dark dusty rose
75		3733	Dusty rose
161		3760	Medium wedgewood
928		3761	Light sky blue (2 skeins)
236		3799	Very dark pewter gray
118		3807	Cornflower blue

CROSS-STITCH (3X)

ANCHOR		DMC	COLORS
306		3820	Dark straw
305		3821	Straw
295		3822	Light straw

BACKSTITCH (1X)

ANCHOR		DMC	COLORS
59	—	150	Ultra very dark dusty rose*
403	—	310	Black* (birds' eyes and beaks)
162	—	517	Dark wedgewood* (forget-me-nots)
308	—	782	Dark topaz* (gold parts of birds)
178	—	791	Very dark cornflower blue* (blue parts of birds)
1044	—	895	Very dark hunter green* (rose leaves)
360	—	898	Very dark coffee brown* (branch, rose stem and tendrils)

FRENCH KNOT (2X)

ANCHOR		DMC	COLORS
275	●	746	Off white* (eyes)

*Duplicate color

Miniature Roses

Design by Lois Winston

Surrounded by stitched "lace," these tiny rosebuds will add graceful style to a hard-to-fill spot in your home.

Materials
- Antique white 28-count Jobelan: 8½ x 8 inches

"Miniature Roses" was stitched on antique white 28-count Jobelan by Wichelt using DMC floss. Finished piece was custom framed.

Skill Level
*Easy

Stitch Count
33 wide x 27 high

Approximate Design Size
11-count 3" x 2½"
14-count 2⅜" x 2"
16-count 2" x 1¾"
18-count 1⅞" x 1½"
22-count 1½" x 1¼"
 28-count over two threads
  2⅜" x 2"

Instructions
1. Center and stitch design on 28-count Jobelan stitching over two threads using three strands floss for Cross-Stitch, two strands floss for Backstitch on stems and one strand floss for remaining Backstitch. ❖

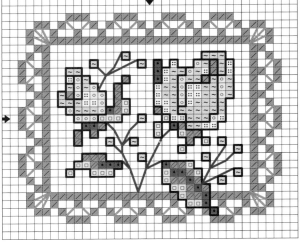

CROSS-STITCH (3X)

ANCHOR		DMC	COLORS
42	◹	309	Dark rose
24	~	776	Medium pink
271	⁛	819	Light baby pink
218	♦	890	Ultra dark pistachio green
52	○	899	Medium rose
244	◿	987	Dark forest green
242	▢	989	Forest green

BACKSTITCH (2X)

ANCHOR		DMC	COLOR
403	▬	310	Black (stems)

BACKSTITCH (1X)

ANCHOR		DMC	COLORS
42	▬	309	Dark rose*
403	▬	310	Black*

Duplicate color

Water Bird

Design by Mike Vickery

The stillness of the morning will surround you while stitching this simple design.

Materials
- Natural 14-count Aida:
  9 x 12½ inches

"Water Bird" was stitched on natural 14-count Aida from Charles Craft using floss from DMC. Finished piece was custom framed.

Skill Level
**Average

Stitch Count
42 wide x 90 high

Approximate Design Size
11-count 3⅞" x 8⅛"
14-count 3" x 6⅜"
16-count 2⅝" x 5⅝"
18-count 2⅜" x 5"
22-count 2" x 4"
28-count over two threads 3" x 6⅜"

Instructions
1. Center and stitch design on 14-count Aida, using two strands floss for Cross-Stitch, and one strand floss for Backstitch. ❖

CROSS-STITCH (2X)

ANCHOR	DMC	COLORS
233	451	Dark shell gray
830	644	Medium beige gray
305	725	Medium light topaz
24	776	Medium pink
23	818	Baby pink
390	822	Light beige gray
397	3023	Light brown gray
266	3347	Medium yellow green
264	3348	Light yellow green
831	3782	Light mocha brown
2	White	White

BACKSTITCH (1X)

ANCHOR	DMC	COLOR
900	648	Light beaver gray

Oriental Poppy Beverage Set

Designs by Hope Murphy

Simple stitching has a bold impact in this easy-to-stitch oriental tea set!

Materials

- Black 14-count Aida:
  18 x 18 inches (for tray)
  2 (6 x 6-inch) pieces (for coasters)
- Black small 9½-inch square tray
- Black 4½-inch-square coaster

"Oriental Poppy Beverage Set" was stitched on black classic reserve 14-count Aida from Charles Craft Inc. using DMC floss. Finished pieces were inserted into square tray #65647 and square coaster #95037 from Sudberry House.

Skill Level
*Easy

Tray Stitch Count
116 wide x 116 high

Approximate Design Size
11-count 10½" x 10½"
14-count 8¼" x 8¼"
16-count 7¼" x 7¼"
18-count 6⅜" x 6⅜"
22-count 5¼" x 5¼"

Coaster Stitch Count
36 wide x 36 high

Approximate Design Size
11-count 3¼" x 3¼"
14-count 2½" x 2½"
16-count 2¼" x 2¼"
18-count 2" x 2"
22-count 3¼" x 3¼"

Instructions
1. Center and stitch design using three strands floss for Cross-Stitch and two strands floss for Backstitch.

Finishing
1. Following manufacturer's instruction, assemble tray and coasters, inserting stitched pieces. ❖

COASTER
CROSS-STITCH (3X)

ANCHOR	DMC	COLORS
289	◩ 307	Lemon
288	+ 445	Light lemon
334	◲ 606	Bright orange red
238	Y 703	Chartreuse

BACKSTITCH (2X)

ANCHOR	DMC	COLORS
403	— 310	Black
43	— 815	Medium garnet
1044	— 895	Very dark hunter green

*Duplicate color

TRAY
CROSS-STITCH (3X)

ANCHOR	DMC	COLORS
289	◩ 307	Lemon
288	+ 445	Light lemon
334	◲ 606	Bright orange red
238	Y 703	Chartreuse

BACKSTITCH (2X)

ANCHOR	DMC	COLOR
1044	— 895	Very dark hunter green

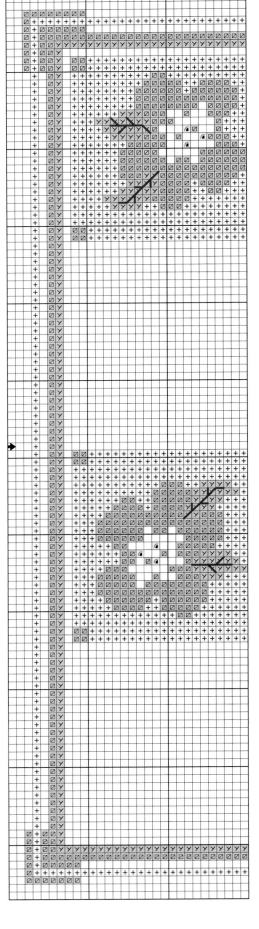

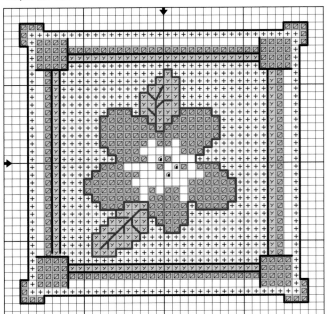

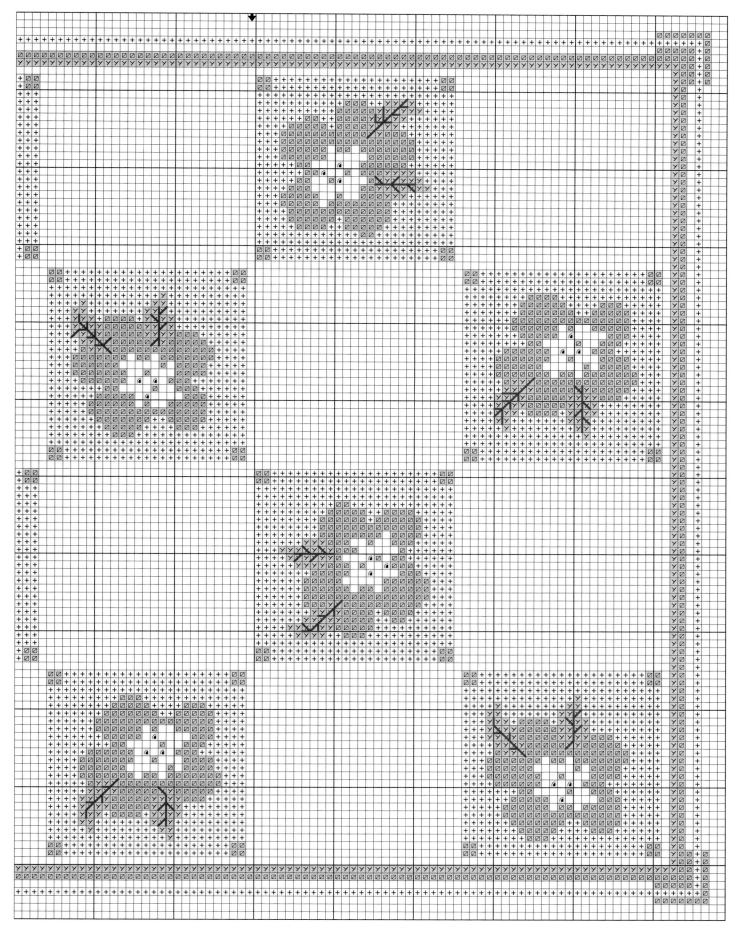

Rose
Heart

Design by Roberta Rankin

Remind your mother how much she means to you by stitching this graceful rose wreath and giving it to her for Valentine's Day!

Materials
- White 25-count Lugana:
  9 x 9 inches

"Rose Heart" was stitched on white 25-count Lugana by Wichelt using DMC floss. Finished piece was custom framed.

Skill Level
*Easy

Stitch Count
39 wide x 34 high

Approximate Design Size
11-count 3½" x 3"
14-count 2¾" x 2⅜"
16-count 2⅜" x 2⅛"
18-count 2⅛" x 1⅞"
22-count 1¾" x 1½"
25-count over two threads 3⅛" x 2¾"

Instructions
1. Center and stitch design on 25-count Lugana, stitching over two threads using two strands floss for Cross-Stitch and one strand floss for Backstitch. ❖

CROSS-STITCH (2X)

ANCHOR		DMC	COLORS
118	•	340	Medium blue violet
117	−	341	Light blue violet
288	>	445	Light lemon
300	□	745	Light pale yellow
24	/	776	Medium pink
271	♡	819	Light baby pink
40	=	956	Geranium
50	○	957	Pale geranium
73	△	963	Ultra very light dusty rose

CROSS-STITCH (2X)

ANCHOR		DMC	COLORS
243	I	988	Medium forest green
268	●	3345	Dark hunter green
264	∷	3348	Light yellow green
120	~	3747	Very light blue violet

BACKSTITCH (1X)

ANCHOR		DMC	COLORS
118	—	340	Medium blue violet*
20	—	816	Garnet

*Duplicate color

Butterfly Table Topper

Design by Pamela Kellogg

Because this lovely table topper comes prefinished, you'll be ready to display this striking piece as soon as you're finished stitching!

Materials
- Ivory 20-count linen table topper
- Glass seed beads:
  2 packets shimmering lilac #02084
  1 packet crystal honey #02019
- 1 packet ivory creme #62039 frosted glass beads

"Butterfly Table Topper" was stitched on ivory 20-count linen Austria table topper #14037/02 by Brunner Haus using Kreinik Silk Mori silk floss, and Mill Hill glass beads.

Skill Level
**Average

Outside Corners Stitch Count
38 wide x 38 high

Approximate Design Size
11-count 3½" x 3½"
14-count 2¾" x 2¾"
16-count 2⅜" x 2⅜"
18-count 2⅛" x 2⅛"
20-count over two threads 4" x 4"
22-count 1¾" x 1¾"

Rectangles Stitch Count
137 wide x 38 high

Approximate Design Size
11-count 12½" x 3½"
14-count 9¾" x 2¾"
16-count 8½" x 2⅜"
18-count 7⅝" x 2⅛"
20-count over two threads 13¾" x 4"
22-count 6¼" x 1¾"

Inside Corners Stitch Count
62 wide x 62 high

Approximate Design Size
11-count 5⅝" x 5⅝"
14-count 4⅜" x 4⅜"
16-count 3⅞" x 3⅞"
18-count 3½" x 3½"
20-count over two threads 6" x 6"
22-count 2⅞" x 2⅞"

Instructions
Note: Silk Mori silk floss is not colorfast; dry-clean only.

1. Center and stitch design, stitching over two threads, and using four strands floss for Cross-Stitch, two strands floss for French Knot and one strand floss for Backstitch. Attach beads using two strands soft white #8000 Silk Mori. See Bead Attachment illustration on page 136. ❖

CROSS-STITCH (4X)

DMC		KREINIK SILK MORI	COLORS
744	=	2024	Medium buttercup (2 skeins)
743	⌐	2026	Dark buttercup
742	✕	2027	Very dark buttercup (2 skeins)
741	♡	2063	Light pumpkin
740	Y	2066	Dark pumpkin
504	::	4162	Lightest Victorian green (5 skeins)
503	X	4163	Light Victorian green (4 skeins)
502	O	4164	Medium Victorian green (2 skeins)
501	✳	4166	Dark Victorian green (2 skeins)
500	⋈	4167	Very dark Victorian green (3 skeins)
552	~	6083	Light grape (3 skeins)
550	⅃	6086	Dark grape (3 skeins)
210	◐	6104	Medium lavender (2 skeins)
209	⊘	6106	Dark lavender (5 skeins)
553	◭	6107	Very dark lavender (4 skeins)
White	·	8000	Soft white (3 skeins)
310	▣	8050	Black (5 skeins)
415	☆	8073	Light charcoal (2 skeins)
413	♥	8075	Medium dark charcoal (2 skeins)

BACKSTITCH (1X)

DMC		KREINIK SILK MORI	COLORS
500	—	4167	Very dark Victorian green*
550	—	6086	Dark grape*
310	—	8050	Black*

FRENCH KNOT (2X)

DMC		KREINIK SILK MORI	COLOR
310	●	8050	Black*

ATTACH BEAD

MILL HILL GLASS BEAD

02019	◯	Crystal honey, attach with 8000 soft white (2X)
02084	●	Shimmering lilac, attach with 8000 soft white (2X)
62039	◯	Ivory creme, attach with 8000 soft white (2X)

Duplicate color

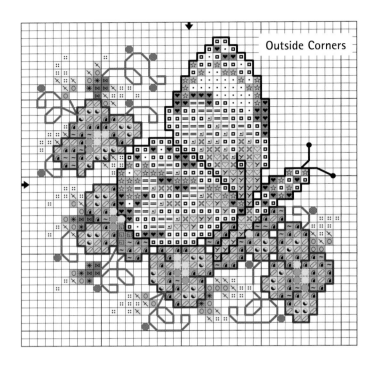

Outside Corners

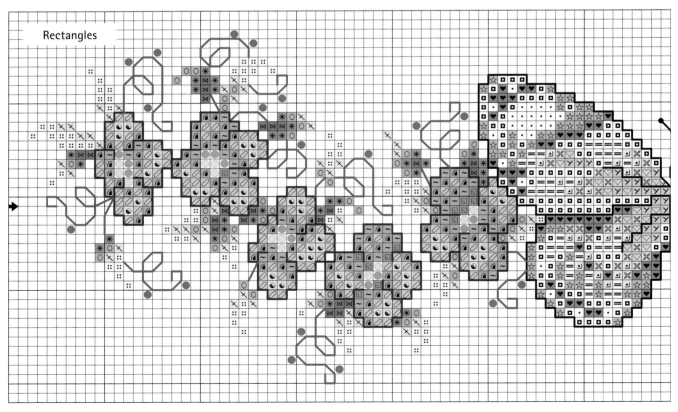

Rectangles

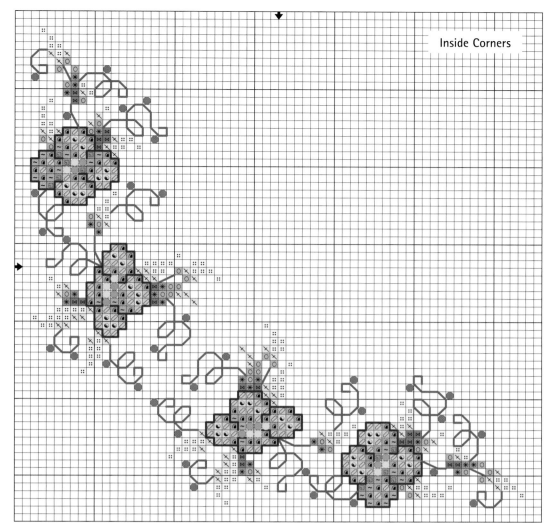

Inside Corners

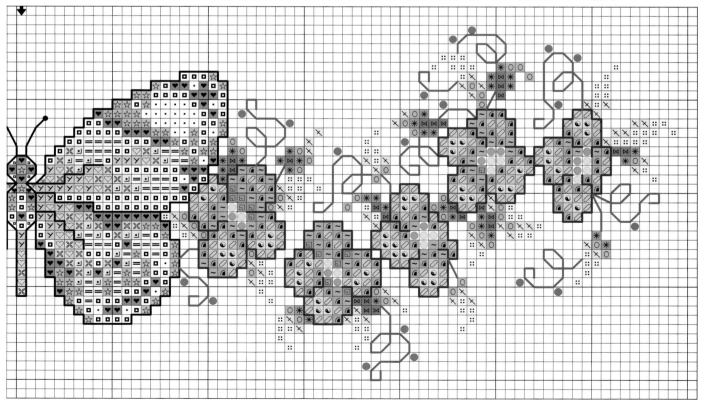

Sweetheart Roses

Designs by Laura Kramer Doyle

A beautiful rose stitched on 14-count plastic canvas makes a great case and cover combo for your purse!

Materials
• Two 8¼ x 11-inch sheets of 14-count perforated plastic canvas

Sweetheart "Roses" projects were stitched using DMC floss.

Skill Level
**Average

Eyeglass Case Front & Back Stitch Count
54 wide x 95 high (each)

Approximate Design Size
11-count 5⅛" x 8⅞"
14-count 4" x 7"
16-count 3½" x 6⅛"
18-count 3⅛" x 5⅜"
22-count 2⅝" x 4½"

Checkbook Front & Back Stitch Count
49 wide x 90 high (each)

Approximate Design Size
11-count 8⅜" x 4¾"
14-count 6⅝" x 3¾"
16-count 5¾" x 3¼"
18-count 5⅛" x 2⅞"
22-count 4¼" x 2⅜"

Checkbook Flap Stitch Count
29 wide x 90 high (each)

Approximate Design Size
11-count 2⅝" x 4¾"

14-count 2" x 3¾"
16-count 1¾" x 3¼"
18-count 1⅝" x 2⅞"
22-count 1⅜" x 2⅜"

Instructions
1. For eyeglasses case, cut two pieces of canvas each 56 holes wide x 97 holes high. Center and stitch Eyeglasses Front and Eyeglasses Back onto canvas pieces using two strands floss for Cross-Stitch.

2. For checkbook front and back, cut two pieces of canvas each 51 holes high by 92 holes wide for front and back (A and B pieces). Center and stitch Checkbook Front and Checkbook Back onto 51-hole x 92-hole pieces of canvas using two strands floss for Cross-Stitch.

3. For checkbook flap, cut one piece of canvas 31 holes high by 92 holes wide (C piece). Center and stitch design using two strands floss.

Finishing
1. For eyeglasses case, hold front and back pieces wrong sides together. Whipstitch (see illustration) pieces together around sides and bottom edges using two strands medium rose floss. Overcast (see illustration) top edge using two strands floss.

2. For checkbook cover, hold A, B and C pieces wrong sides together according to Assembly Diagram. Whipstitch together using two strands medium pink floss. Fold inner flap C piece onto B piece (wrong sides will be together). Overcast all outer edges using two strands medium pink floss. ❖

Assembly Diagram
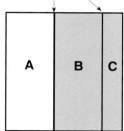

CROSS-STITCH (2X)

ANCHOR		DMC	COLORS
42		309	Dark rose
302		743	Medium yellow
300		745	Light pale yellow
24		776	Medium pink
307		783	Medium topaz
43		815	Medium garnet
271		819	Light baby pink
52		899	Medium rose
268		3345	Dark hunter green
266		3347	Medium yellow green
264		3348	Light yellow green
2		White	White

Checkbook Cover Front (A)

CROSS-STITCH (2X)

ANCHOR	DMC	COLORS
42	309	Dark rose
302	743	Medium yellow
300	745	Light pale yellow
24	776	Medium pink
307	783	Medium topaz
43	815	Medium garnet
271	819	Light baby pink
52	899	Medium rose
268	3345	Dark hunter green
266	3347	Medium yellow green
264	3348	Light yellow green
2	White	White

Checkbook Flap (C)

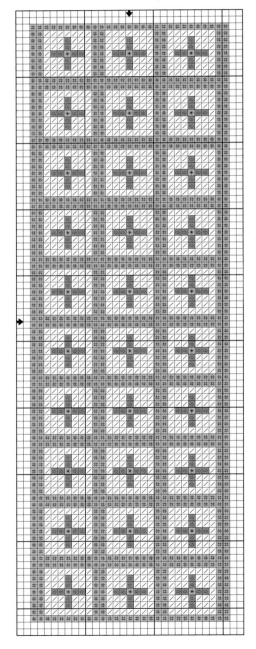

Eyeglass Case Front

Whipstitch

Overcast

Eyeglass Case Back

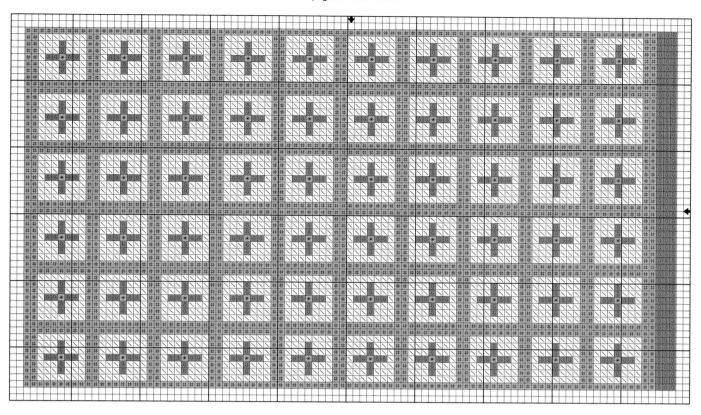

Checkbook Cover Back (B)

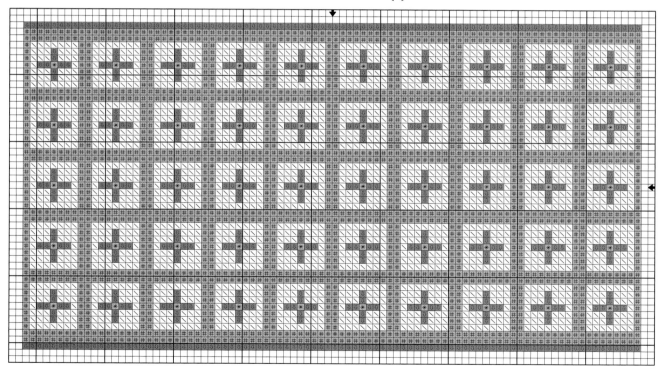

Flower Boxes

Designs by Dayna Stedry

Bring a breeze of spring into your home or that of a friend with a trendy box of blooms.

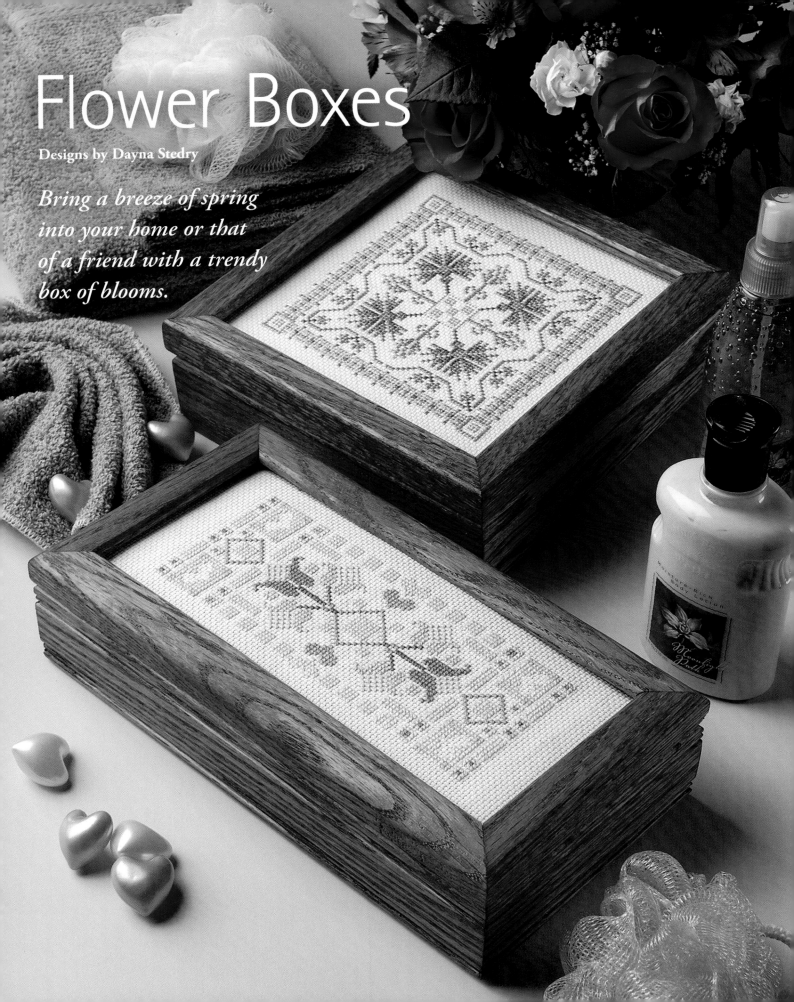

Materials

- Ivory 14-count Aida:
  11 x 11 inches (for Thistle)
  9 x 14 inches (for Tulips)
- Wooden box:
  5½ x 5½-inch design opening
    (for Thistle)
  3½ x 7½-inch design opening (for Tulips)

"Flower Boxes" projects were stitched using DMC floss.

Skill Level
**Average

Tulips Stitch Count
43 wide x 99 high

Approximate Design Size
11-count 4" x 9"
14-count 3½" x 7⅛"
16-count 2¾" x 6¼"
18-count 2⅜" x 5½"
22-count 2" x 4½"

Thistle Stitch Count
75 wide x 75 high

Approximate Design Size
11-count 6⅞" x 6⅞"
14-count 5⅜" x 5⅜"
16-count 4¾" x 4¾"
18-count 4¼" x 4¼"
22-count 3½" x 3½"

Instructions

1. Center and stitch design of choice using two strands floss for Cross-Stitch and Backstitch.

Finishing

1. Position and secure design in box following manufacturer's instructions. ❖

TULIPS
CROSS-STITCH (2X)

ANCHOR		DMC	COLORS
215	↑	320	Medium pistachio green
8	*	353	peach
261	●	368	Light pistachio green
1043	✓	369	Very light pistachio green
891	✖	676	Light old gold
886	▶	677	Very light old gold
1022	‹	760	Salmon
1021	℘	761	Light salmon
1023	⊠	3712	Medium salmon
1020	☆	3713	Very light salmon

Tulips

THISTLES

CROSS-STITCH (2X)

ANCHOR	DMC	COLORS
860	522	Fern green
858	524	Very light fern green
886	677	Very light old gold
1033	932	Light antique blue
871	3041	Medium antique violet
870	3042	Light antique violet
869	3743	Very light antique violet

CROSS-STITCH (2X)

ANCHOR	DMC	COLORS
1032	3752	Very light antique blue
1031	3753	Ultra very light antique blue
2	3865	Winter white

BACKSTITCH (2X)

ANCHOR	DMC	COLOR
1032	3752	Very light antique blue*

*Duplicate color

Thistles

Bloomin' Blazes

Design by Annette Rogers

The mandala feel to the design of this pillow is suitable for many types of decor. Working over three threads of fabric gives a different stitching experience!

Materials

- White 20-count Lugana:
  20 x 20 inches
- 16-inch pillow form
- 17-inch square backing fabric
- 2 yards piping cord
- Zipper (optional)

"Bloomin' Blazes" was stitched on white 20-count Lugana by Zweigart using Anchor floss.

Skill Level
**Average

Stitch Count
94 wide x 94 high

Approximate Design Size
11-count 8½" x 8½"
14-count 6¾" x 6¾"
16-count 5⅞" x 5⅞"
18-count 5¼" x 5¼"
20-count over three threads 14" x 14"
22-count 4¼" x 4¼"

Instructions

1. Center and stitch design, stitching over three threads using six strands floss for Cross-Stitch and three strands floss for Backstitch. Use six strands floss wrapped once for French Knot.

Finishing
Note: *Use a ½-inch seam allowance.*

1. Trim stitched piece to 17 inches square. With right sides facing, pin backing fabric and stitched front together, placing piping between the two layers of fabric with raw edge of piping facing the outside edge of pillow. Sew layers together with a zipper foot against piping, leaving top edge open for inserting a zipper or for turning.

2. If using a zipper, stitch in place and turn pillow right side out. If not using a zipper, turn pillow right side out; insert pillow form and sew opening closed using invisible stitches that also tack piping in place. ❖

CROSS-STITCH (6X)

DMC		ANCHOR	COLORS
3350		59	Ultra dark dusty rose
3805		62	Cyclamen pink
963		73	Ultra very light dusty rose (2 skeins)
3354		74	Light dusty rose
3733		75	Dusty rose
799		136	Medium delft blue (2 skeins)
813		140	Light blue
828		158	Ultra very light blue
472		254	Ultra light avocado green (2 skeins)
470		266	Light avocado green (4 skeins)
937		268	Medium avocado green (5 skeins)
934		269	Black avocado green (5 skeins)
712		275	Cream (3 skeins)
745		300	Light pale yellow
744		301	Pale yellow (2 skeins)
972		302	Deep canary
743		305	Medium yellow (2 skeins)
608		330	Bright orange
3823		386	Ultra pale yellow

BACKSTITCH (3X)

DMC		ANCHOR	COLORS
799		136	Medium delft blue*
813		140	Light blue*
472		254	Ultra light avocado green*
470		266	Light avocado green*
972		302	Deep canary*
608		330	Bright orange*

FRENCH KNOT (6X)

DMC		ANCHOR	COLORS
3350		59	Ultra dark dusty rose*
3731		76	Very dark dusty rose

*Duplicate color

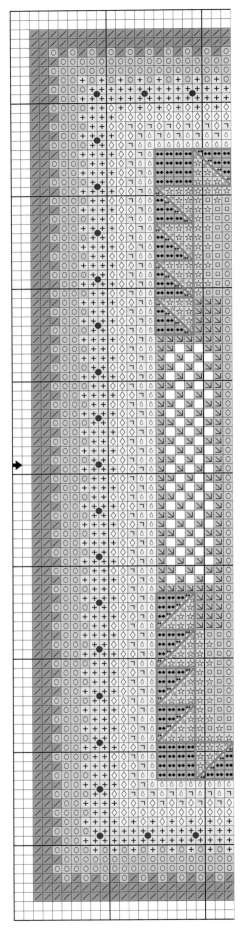

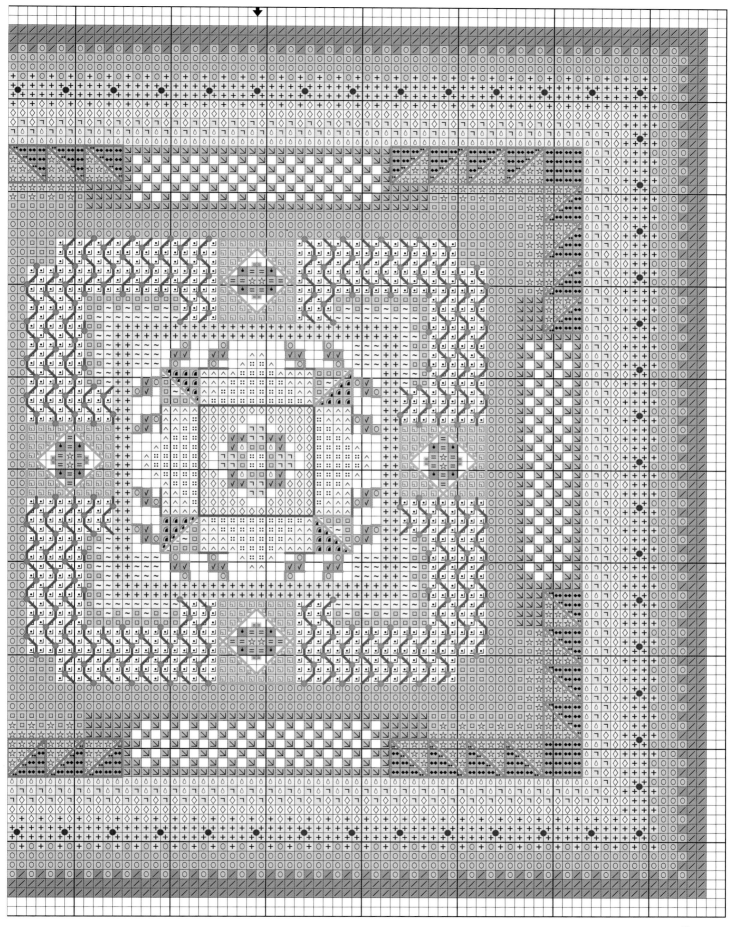

Blue Bells

Design by Kathleen Hurley

Create a floral photo mat for the fresh
"picks" from your family garden!

Materials
- White 22-count Vienna:
  14 x 16 inches
- Photos of choice

*"Blue Bells" was stitched on white 22-count Vienna by Wichelt Imports Inc. using DMC floss. Finished piece was custom framed.

Skill Level
**Average

Stitch Count
80 wide x 104 high

Approximate Design Size
11-count 7⅜" x 9½"
14-count 5¾" x 7½"
16-count 5" x 6½"
18-count 4½" x 5⅞"
22-count 3⅝" x 4¾"
22-count over two threads 7⅜" x 9½"

Instructions
1. Center and stitch design, stitching over two threads and using four strands floss for Cross-Stitch and two strands floss for Backstitch and French Knot.

Finishing
1. Trim photos to fit and mount in open areas. ❖

CROSS-STITCH (4X)
ANCHOR		DMC	COLORS
226	⊥	702	Kelly green
256	«	704	Bright chartreuse
926	::	712	Cream
387	✿	739	Ultra very light tan
131	◆	798	Dark delft blue
130	✳	809	Delft blue

BACKSTITCH (2X)
ANCHOR		DMC	COLORS
923	—	699	Green
134	—	820	Very dark royal blue
381	—	938	Ultra dark coffee brown
297	—	973	Bright canary

FRENCH KNOT (2X)
ANCHOR		DMC	COLORS
297	●	973	Bright canary*

*Duplicate color

Hearts & Flowers

Design by Polly Carbonari

This sweet pillow makes a romantic statement in a cottage bedroom.

Materials

- Pearl 25-count Linen 15 x 15-inches
- 12-inch pillow form
- ½ yard fabric
- 1½ yards 1-inch-wide rickrack

"Hearts & Flowers" was stitched using DMC floss.

Skill Level

**Average

Stitch Count

107 wide x 107 high

Approximate Design Size

11-count 9¾" x 9¾"
14-count 7¾" x 7¾"
16-count 6¾" x 6¾"
18-count 6" x 6"
22-count 5" x 5"
25-count over two threads 8⅝" x 8⅝"

Instructions

1. Center and stitch design, stitching over two threads and using two strands floss for Cross-Stitch.

Finishing

1. Trim design to 13½ inches square.

2. From fabric, cut two 9 x 13½-inch pieces for back and one 4 x 104-inch piece for ruffle (piecing as necessary).

3. With right sides together, using ½-inch seam allowance, sew shorts ends of 4 x 104-inch fabric together, forming ring. Fold wrong sides facing; press. Gather unfinished edge to fit around outside edges of front. With right sides facing, sew first rickrack, then ruffle to front.

4. Hem one 13½-inch edge of each back piece. Place one hemmed edge over the other, overlapping enough to create a 13½ x 13½-inch back with opening. Baste outside edges together; press.

5. With right sides facing, sew front and back together. Trim seam and turn right side out; press. Insert pillow form. ❖

CROSS-STITCH (2X)

ANCHOR		DMC	COLORS
119	◣	156	Medium light blue violet
117	♦♦	341	Light blue violet
08	#	353	Peach
256	○	704	Bright chartreuse
295	⁒	726	Light topaz
259	+	772	Very light yellow green
160	6	827	Very light blue
186	m	993	Very light aquamarine
887	)	3046	Medium yellow beige
264	2	3348	Light yellow green
87	↑	3607	Light plum
86	−	3608	Very light plum
85	$	3609	Ultra light plum
869	╱	3743	Very light antique violet
120	·	3747	Very light blue violet
928	(	3761	Light sky blue

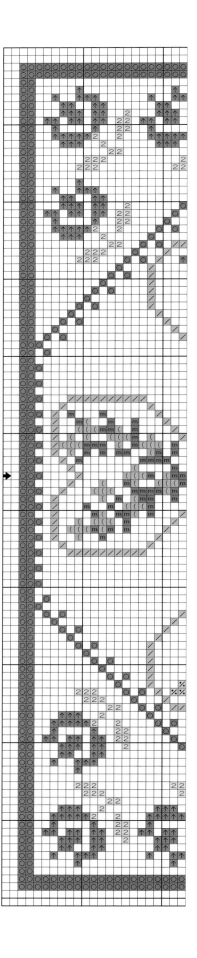

Sunflowers

Design by Pamela Kellogg

Sunflowers and butterfly wings glisten in the early autumn sun with the addition of metallic blending filament to the stitches.

Materials
- Forget-me-not blue 28-count linen: 12 x 13½ inches

"Sunflowers" was stitched on forget-me-not blue 28-count linen from Wichelt using DMC floss and Kreinik blending filament.

Skill Level
**Average

Stitch Count
56 wide x 76 high

Approximate Design Size
11-count 5" x 7"
14-count 4" x 5⅜"
16-count 3½" x 4¾"
18-count 3" x 4¼"
22-count 2½" x 3½"

Instructions
1. Center and stitch design on linen, stitching over two threads and using three strands floss, or two strands floss and one strand blending filament held together for Cross-Stitch, and one strand floss for Backstitch. Use one strand floss for French Knot, wrapping needle twice. ❖

CROSS-STITCH (3X)

ANCHOR		DMC	COLORS
120		157	Very light cornflower blue
403		310	Black
400		317	Pewter gray
401		413	Dark pewter gray
358		433	Medium brown
310		434	Light brown
1046		435	Very light brown
1045		436	Tan
362		437	Light tan
326		720	Dark orange spice
324		721	Medium orange spice
275		746	Off white
259		772	Very light yellow green
307		783	Medium topaz
941		792	Dark cornflower blue
176		793	Medium cornflower blue
175		794	Light cornflower blue
359		801	Dark coffee brown
1044		895	Very dark hunter green
360		898	Very dark coffee brown
340		919	Red copper
1004		920	Medium copper
381		938	Ultra dark coffee brown
292		3078	Very light golden yellow
268		3345	Dark hunter green
267		3346	Hunter green
266		3347	Medium yellow green
264		3348	Light yellow green
236		3799	Very dark pewter gray
118		3807	Cornflower blue
306		3820	Dark straw
305		3821	Straw
295		3822	Light straw
275		3823	Ultra pale yellow
1002		3854	Medium autumn gold
301		3855	Light autumn gold

KREINIK BLENDED CROSS-STITCH

ANCHOR		DMC	COLORS
120		157	Very light cornflower blue* (2X) with 093 star mauve BF (1X)
941		792	Dark cornflower blue* (2X) with 093 star mauve* BF (1X)
176		793	Medium cornflower blue* (2X) with 093 star mauve* BF (1X)
175		794	Light cornflower blue* (2X) with 093 star mauve* BF (1X)
118		3807	Cornflower blue* (2X) with 093 star mauve* BF (1X)
1002		3854	Medium antique gold* (1X) with 324/721 medium orange spice* (1X) and 093 star mauve* BF (1X)

BACKSTITCH (1X)

ANCHOR		DMC	COLORS
120	—	157	Very light cornflower blue*
403	—	310	Black*
308	—	782	Dark topaz
1044	—	895	Very dark hunter green*
340	—	918	Dark red cooper

FRENCH KNOT (1X)

ANCHOR		DMC	COLORS
403	●	310	Black*
275	●	746	Off white*

*Duplicate color

Antique House Sampler

Design by Carla Acosta

Use overdyed floss for the look of color changes without the work!

Materials
- Café mocha 32-count country French Linen: 15 x 17½ inches
- Graph paper
- Colored pencils or markers

"Antique House Sampler" was stitched on café mocha 32-count country French linen by Wichelt Imports Inc. using floss from The Gentle Arts Sampler Threads. Finished piece was custom framed.

Skill Level
*Easy

Stitch Count
145 wide x 181 high

Approximate Design Size
11-count 13⅛" x 16½"
14-count 10⅜" x 13"
16-count 9" x 11⅜"
18-count 8" x 10"
22-count 6½" x 8¼"
32-count over two threads 9" x 11⅜"

Instructions
Note: Choose desired letters and numbers from graph for initials and date. Chart onto graph paper for proper placement.

1. Center and stitch design on 32-count country French linen, stitching over two threads using two strands floss for Cross-Stitch and Backstitch. Use two strands floss (wrapped twice) for French Knot.

Using Sampler Threads

The use of hand-painted or overdyed floss will allow you to create subtle shading stitch by stitch. There are several terms associated with the process used to create these fibers:

Variegated—Typically, mechanically done, measured sections of color are created by graduating the shading from light hued to dark hued within a color family.

Space dyed—Gradient color hues ranging from lightest shades to very dark shades.

Shadow dyed—A darker color is applied to a previously dyed fiber to create the illusion of a shadowed surface.

Overdyed—A system of dying one color on top of, or over, a previously dyed color in an unevenly spaced manner. This method is done by hand and creates the depth of color evident in this design.

Here are a few tips to help you make the most of the built-in color changes that overdyed floss can provide to your work:

Don't pull the floss too tight, as this will cause bunching in the fabric, especially with the heavier fibers.

When stitching with overdyed fibers, complete each stitch as you go to receive the full effect of the different color shades. If a more mottled effect is desired, work the first half of the stitches across the row, and complete the stitches by working back across that row.

For yet another shaded look, complete every other stitch in a row, leaving an unworked stitch. Then return across the row, working in the purposely created holes.

If stitching with two or more strands of floss, reverse the direction of one of the strands when threading the needle. This gives a tweedy look to the stitching. ❖

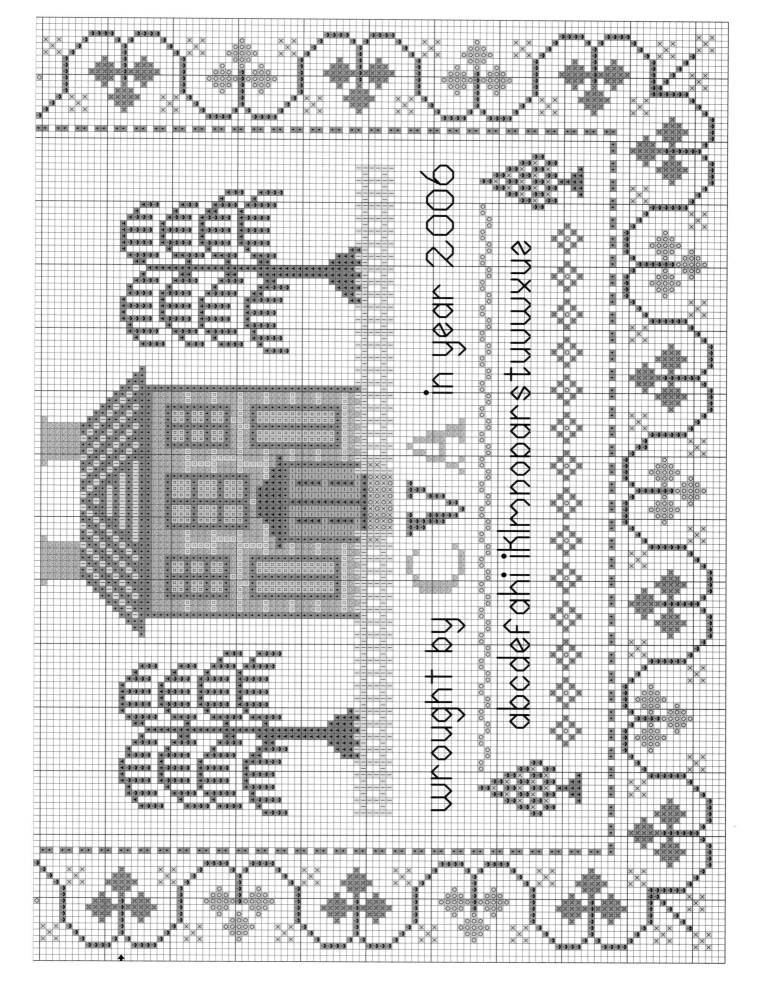

Psalm 63:7

Design by Cathy Bussi

Stitch this beautiful sampler to express your joy in the Lord.

Materials
- Antique white 32-count Linen:
  10 x 13 inches

"Psalm 63:7" was stitched with DMC floss. Finished piece was custom framed.

Skill Level
**Average

Stitch Count
66 wide x 107 high

Approximate Design Size
11-count 6" x 9¾"
14-count 4¾" x 7¾"
16-count 4⅛" x 6¾"
18-count 3¾" x 6"
22-count 3" x 4⅞"
32-count over two threads 4⅛" x 6¾"

Instructions
Note: Select desired letters for initials from alphabet graph.

1. Center and stitch design, stitching over two threads and using two strands floss or one strand floss as indicated on key for Cross-Stitch. Use one strand floss for Backstitch, Elongated Eyelet, Eyelet, Herringbone Stitch, Four-sided Stitch and French Knot (see Special Stitches.) ❖

CROSS-STITCH (2X)

ANCHOR	DMC	COLORS
858	524	Very light fern green
390	822	Light beige gray
4146	950	Light desert sand
391	3033	Very light mocha brown
260	3364	Pine green
1009	3770	Very light tawny
1008	3773	Medium desert sand
778	3774	Very light desert sand
831	3782	Light mocha brown

CROSS-STITCH (1X)

ANCHOR	DMC	COLORS
262	3363	Medium pine green
260	3364	Pine green*

BACKSTITCH (1X)

ANCHOR	DMC	COLORS
392	642	Dark beige gray
4146	950	Light desert sand*
262	3363	Medium pine green*
260	3364	Pine green*
831	3782	Light mocha brown*

ELONGATED EYELET (1X)

ANCHOR	DMC	COLOR
858	524	Very light fern green*

EYELET (1X)

ANCHOR	DMC	COLORS
390	822	Light beige gray*
4146	950	Light desert sand*

HERRINGBONE STITCH (1X)

ANCHOR	DMC	COLOR
1008	3773	Medium desert sand*

FOUR-SIDED STITCH (1X)

ANCHOR	DMC	COLOR
390	822	Light beige gray*

FRENCH KNOT (1X)

ANCHOR	DMC	COLORS
392	642	Dark beige gray*
262	3363	Medium pine green*

*Duplicate color

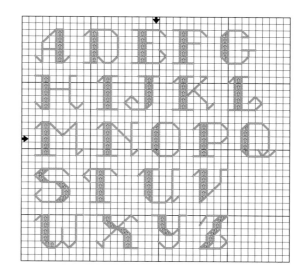

Herringbone Stitch (Hb)

Eyelet (Eye)

Elongated Eyelet

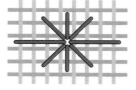

Four-sided Stitch

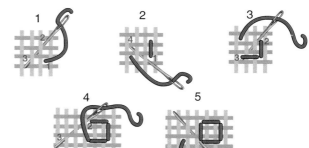

Work from right to left and stitch over four threads in each direction. (1) To start, come up at 1, go in at 2, exit at 3. (2) Go in at 1 and come up at 4. (3) Go in a 2, exit at 3. (4) Finally go in at 2, exit at 3 (last bar of first Four-sided Stitch forms first bar of second stitch). (5) Repeat steps 1-4 until row is completed. Pull each stitch tight.

CROSS-STITCH (2X)

ANCHOR		DMC	COLORS
858	⊗⊗	524	Very light fern green
390	▢	822	Light beige gray
4146	⬆	950	Light desert sand
391	◖	3033	Very light mocha brown
260	⊟	3364	Pine green
1009	⠿	3770	Very light tawny
1008	◪	3773	Medium desert sand
778	☆	3774	Very light desert sand
831	⊠	3782	Light mocha brown

CROSS-STITCH (1X)

ANCHOR		DMC	COLORS
262	◪	3363	Medium pine green
260	△	3364	Pine green*

BACKSTITCH (1X)

ANCHOR		DMC	COLORS
392	—	642	Dark beige gray
4146	—	950	Light desert sand*
262	—	3363	Medium pine green*
260	—	3364	Pine green*
831	—	3782	Light mocha brown*

ELONGATED EYELET (1X)

ANCHOR		DMC	COLOR
858	—	524	Very light fern green*

EYELET (1X)

ANCHOR		DMC	COLORS
390	—	822	Light beige gray*
4146	—	950	Light desert sand*

HERRINGBONE STITCH (1X)

ANCHOR		DMC	COLOR
1008	—	3773	Medium desert sand*

FOUR-SIDED STITCH (1X)

ANCHOR		DMC	COLOR
390	—	822	Light beige gray*

FRENCH KNOT (1X)

ANCHOR		DMC	COLORS
392	●	642	Dark beige gray*
262	●	3363	Medium pine green*

*Duplicate color

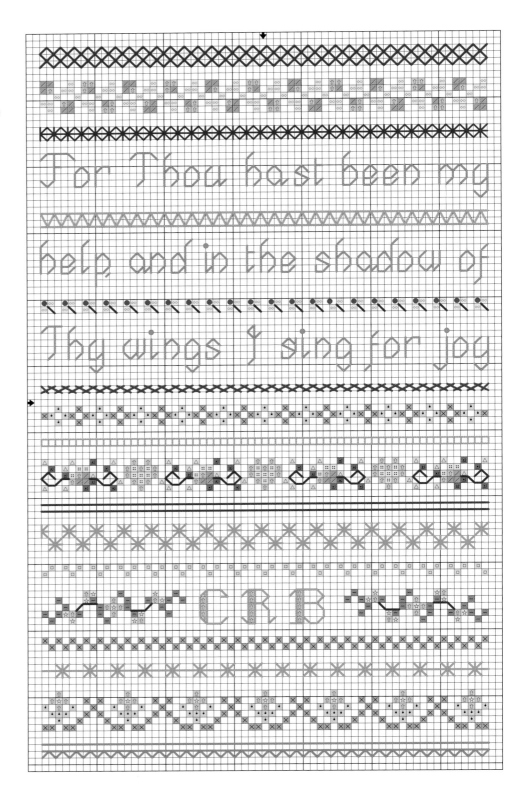

Garden Friends Sampler

Design by Janelle Giese

Buttons and interesting stitches provide dimension to a happy autumn sampler.

CROSS-STITCH (3X)

ANCHOR		DMC	COLORS
897	+	221	Very dark shell pink
352	◆◆	300	Very dark mahogany
1049	#	301	Medium mahogany
351	◿	400	Dark mahogany
1046	%	435	Very light brown
362	♣	437	Light tan
267	◪	469	Avocado green
265	::	471	Very light avocado green
891	○	676	Light old gold
275	⌐	746	Off white
1012	∕	754	Light peach
882	⊕	758	Very light terra cotta
1022	♡	760	Salmon
307	△	783	Medium topaz
360	✕	839	Dark beige brown
379	▪	840	Medium beige brown
1033	⤬	932	Light antique blue
1048	∩	3776	Light mahogany
393	З	3787	Dark brown gray
311	∧	3827	Pale golden brown

CROSS-STITCH (1X)

ANCHOR		DMC	COLORS
1049	✿	301	Medium mahogany*
351	▣	400	Dark mahogany*
1046	◎	435	Very light brown*
267	∥	469	Avocado green*
265	✤	471	Very light avocado green*
891	✛	676	Light old gold*
307	≋	783	Medium topaz*
1048	◁	3776	Light mahogany*

COMPOUND CROSS-STITCH

ANCHOR		DMC	COLORS
1046	✕	435	Very light brown* (3X) with 265/471 very light avocado green* (1X)
891	▼	676	Light old gold* (3X) with 1046/435 very light brown* (1X)
275	✳	746	Off white* (3X) with 267/469 avocado green* (1X)
275	၈	746	Off white* (3X) with 265/471 very light avocado green* (1X)
379	✤	840	Medium beige brown* (3X) with 267/469 avocado green* (1X)

LAZY-DAISY STITCH (2X)

ANCHOR		DMC	COLOR
1033	▬	932	Light antique blue*

BACKSTITCH (2X)

ANCHOR		DMC	COLOR
382	▬	3371	Black brown

BACKSTITCH (1X)

ANCHOR		DMC	COLORS
861	▬	935	Dark avocado green
382	▬	3371	Black brown*

STRAIGHT STITCH (3X)

ANCHOR		DMC	COLORS
267	▬	469	Avocado green*
311	▬	3827	Pale golden brown*

STRAIGHT STITCH (1X)

ANCHOR		DMC	COLOR
360	▬	839	Dark beige brown*

FRENCH KNOT (1X)

ANCHOR		DMC	COLOR
382	●	3371	Black brown*

*Duplicate color

Materials
- Antique white 28-count Jobelan: 13 x 15 inches
- Mill Hill buttons:
  2 bumblebees #86128
  Marten house #86130

"Garden Friends Sampler" was stitched on antique white 28-count Jobelan by Wichelt using floss from DMC and Mill Hill buttons. Finished piece was custom framed.

Skill Level
**Average

Stitch Count
96 wide x 129 high

Approximate Design Size

11-count 8¾" x 11¾"
14-count 6⅞" x 9"
16-count 6" x 8"
18-count 5¼" x 7"
22-count 4⅜" x 5⅞"
28-count over two
    threads 6⅞" x 9"

Instructions

1. Center and stitch design, stitching over two threads using one strand floss for Cross-Stitch on lettering and numerals, and three strands floss for remaining Cross-Stitch. To work Compound Cross-Stitch, work a one-strand Cross-Stitch over a completed three-strand Cross-Stitch. Use two strands floss for Lazy-Daisy Stitch, one strand or two strands floss for Backstitch, and three strands or one strand floss for Straight Stitch. Use one strand floss for French Knot, wrapping needle twice for eyes and three times for flowers.

Finishing

1. Sew buttons on as shown in photo. ❖

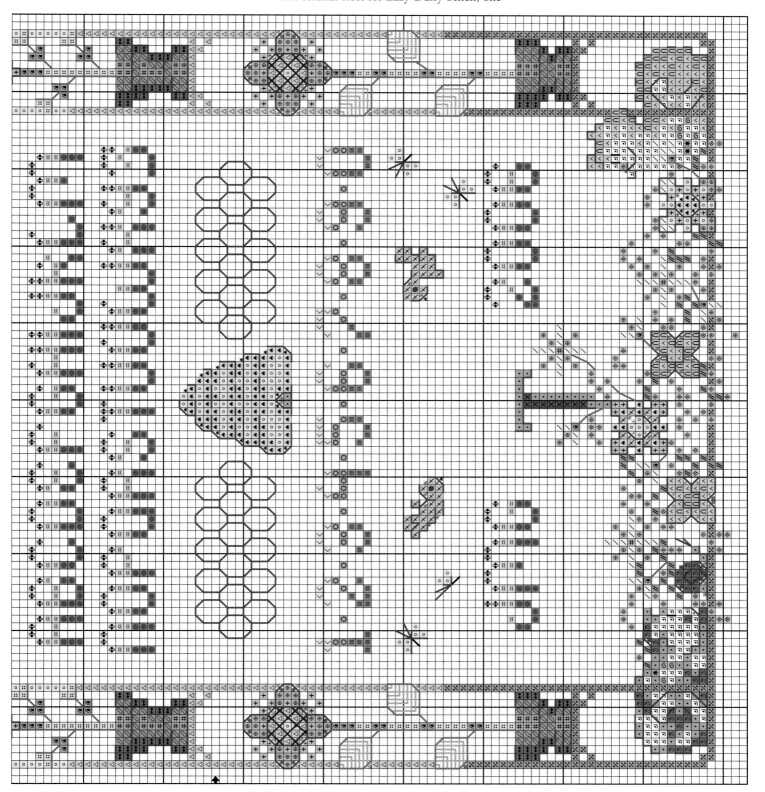

Happiest Heart Sampler

Design by Carla Acosta

This cheery wall hanger will brighten up any room in which it is placed.

Materials
- White 14-count Aida: 16½ x 18½ inches
- ⅔ yard green print fabric
- ⅓ yard burgundy fabric
- 5-inch square light floral fabric
- 16 x 18-inch piece quilt batting

"Happiest Heart Sampler" was stitched on white 14-count Aida from Zweigart using floss from DMC.

Skill Level
**Average

Stitch Count
146 wide x 175 high

Approximate Design Size
11-count 13⅜" x 16"
14-count 10½" x 12½"
16-count 9⅛" x 11"
18-count 8⅛" x 9⅞"
22-count 6⅝" x 8"
28-count over two threads 10½" x 1½"

Instructions
1. Center and stitch design on 14-count Aida, using two strands floss for Cross-Stitch, Backstitch on lowercase lettering and French Knot. Use one strand floss for all other Backstitch.

Finishing
Note: Use ½-inch seam allowance throughout. Trim main design to measure 12 x 14 inches.

1. From burgundy fabric, cut two 2 x 14-inch strips for A pieces, and two 2 x 12-inch strips for B pieces. From light floral fabric, cut four 2 x 2-inch squares for corner pieces.

2. With right sides together, sew one A piece to each side of stitched piece. Press seams toward burgundy fabric. With right sides together, sew a corner piece to each short end of B pieces. Stitch B pieces to top and bottom. Press seams toward burgundy fabric.

3. From green print fabric, cut two 2-inch-wide strips to fit across top and bottom of pieced front; sew in place. Cut two more 2-inch-wide strips from green print fabric to fit across each side of pieced front; sew in place.

4. Also from green print fabric, cut one 16 x 18-inch piece for back, and one 2 x 15-inch strip for rod pocket. On rod-pocket strip, press under ½ inch on one long edge and two short edges.

5. Baste batting to right side of pieced front. With raw edges even and right side facing down, baste rod pocket strip across top of pieced front over batting. With right sides together, baste back to front, sandwiching batting and rod pocket strip between.

6. Sew around outer edges, leaving an opening for turning. Trim seams; turn right side out. Press. Hand-stitch opening closed. Machine-stitch in seams around stitched design.

7. Fold rod pocket strip to back and hand-stitch in place along bottom folded edge. ❖

Front Assembly Diagram

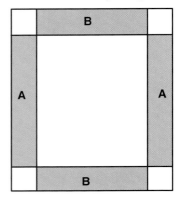

ABCDEFGHIJKLMN
OPQRSTUVWXYZ
12345 67890

CVA
2006

abcdefghijklmnopqrstuvwxyz ❤ the heart
is the happiest when it beats for others

CROSS-STITCH (2X)

ANCHOR		DMC	COLORS
108	◿	210	Medium lavender
342	▢	211	Light lavender
1026	#	225	Ultra very light shell pink
977	♡	334	Medium baby blue
9	T	352	Light coral
8	$	353	Peach
261	▯	368	Light pistachio green
1043	⊡	369	Very light pistachio green
1046	◪	435	Very light brown
891	◁	676	Light old gold
901	☆	680	Dark old gold
890	¢	729	Medium old gold
128	m	775	Very light baby blue
24	✕	776	Medium pink
23	↑	818	Baby pink
206	◇	966	Medium baby green
870	4	3042	Light antique violet
129	◁	3325	Light baby blue
36	2	3326	Light rose
869	α	3743	Very light antique violet
140	V	3755	Baby blue

BACKSTITCH (2X)

ANCHOR		DMC	COLOR
1046	—	435	Very light brown*

BACKSTITCH (1X)

ANCHOR		DMC	COLOR
1046	—	435	Very light brown*

FRENCH KNOT (2X)

ANCHOR		DMC	COLOR
1046	●	435	Very light brown*

Duplicate color

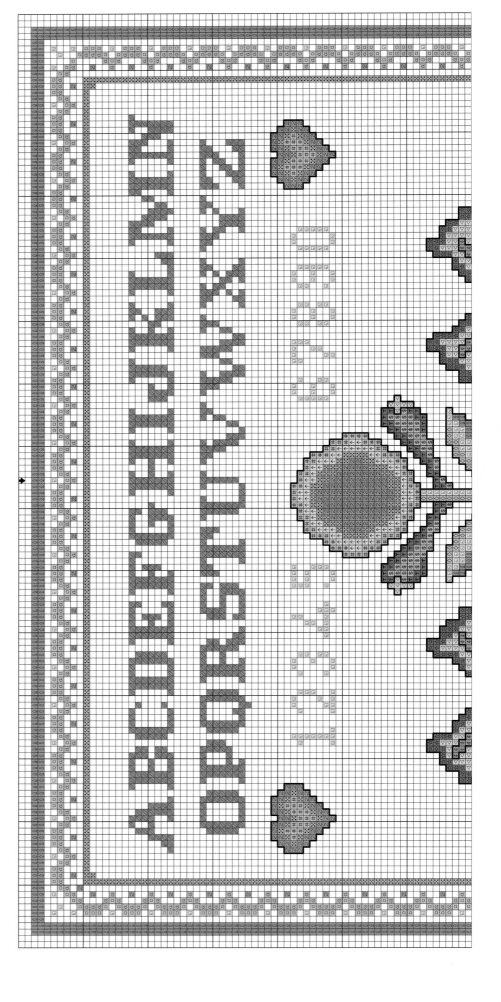

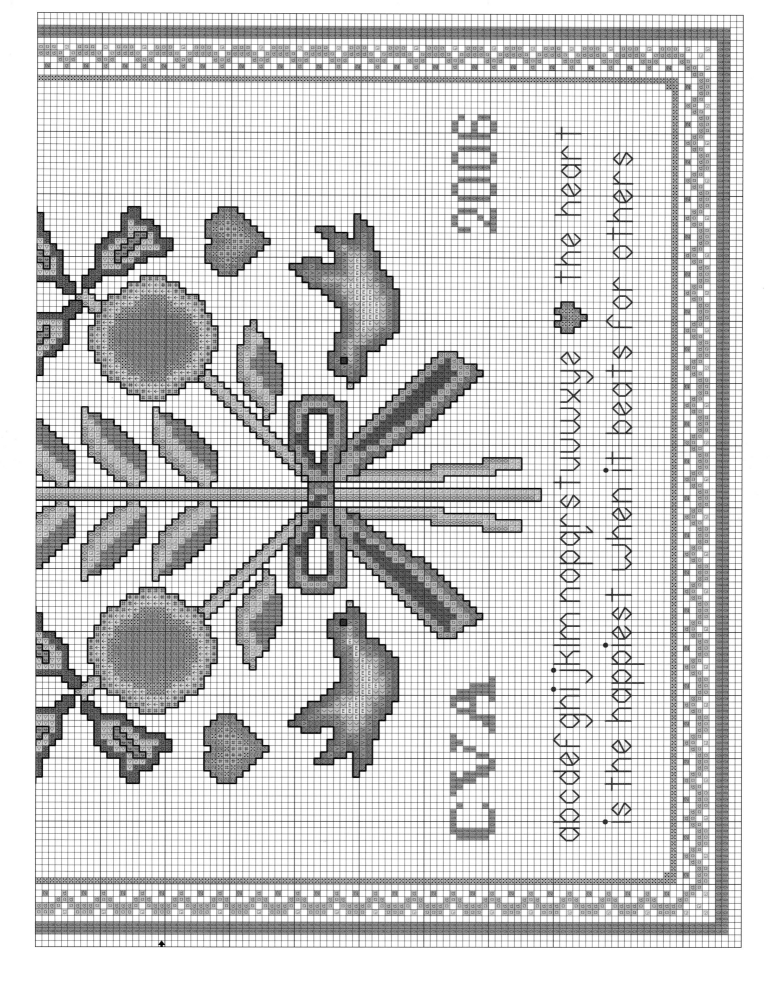

Roses & Thorns

Design by Julia Lucas

This small piece has large visual impact when displayed in a gorgeous mirror frame. The lovely sentiment would also be at home in a box lid.

Materials
- Light rose 14-count Aida: 11 x 11 inches
- Mirror frame

"Roses & Thorns" was stitched on light rose 14-count Aida by Zweigart using DMC floss. Stitched piece is shown in a mirror frame by Olde Colonial Designs.

Approximate Design Size
11-count 3¾" x 3¾"
14-count 3" x 3"
16-count 2½" x 2½"
18-count 2¼" x 2¼"
22-count 1⅞" x 1⅞"

Skill Level
*Easy

Stitch Count
40 wide x 41 high

Instructions
1. Center and stitch design using three strands floss for Cross-Stitch and one strand floss for Backstitch. Use one strand floss for French Knot, wrapping needle twice. ❖

CROSS-STITCH (3X)

ANCHOR	DMC	COLORS
218	319	Very dark pistachio green
217	367	Dark pistachio green
75	962	Medium dusty rose
73	963	Ultra very light dusty rose
59	3350	Ultra dark dusty rose

BACKSTITCH (1X)

ANCHOR	DMC	COLOR
59	3350	Ultra dark dusty rose*

FRENCH KNOT (1X)

ANCHOR	DMC	COLOR
59	3350	Ultra dark dusty rose*

*Duplicate color

Misty Lavender Sampler

Design by Janelle Giese

This exciting sampler offers the opportunity to use many different threads while practicing different stitch techniques! The result? A lovely piece to grace your home with the hint of misty lavender on a Scottish hillside!

Materials

- Antique white 28-count Alma Cloth: 11 x 16 inches
- Kreinik threads and braids:
  Silk Mori: 6123 light dusty lavender, 1092 lightest wood violet
  Silk Serica: 6123 light dusty lavender, 1092 lightest wood violet
  #4 Very Fine Braid: 03 pearl
  #8 Fine Braid: 225 slate, 1223 passion plum
  #12 Tapestry Braid: 001 silver
  1-ply cord: 001 silver, 225 slate
  Kreinik Ombré: 1600 misty lavender
- Mill Hill seed beads: 00161 crystal, 00081 jet

"Misty Lavender Sampler" was stitched on Alma Cloth by Wichelt Imports Inc., using Silk Mori floss, Silk Serica floss, Fine Braid, Very Fine Braid, Tapestry Braid, Cord and Ombré from Kreinik, and Mill Hill Frosted and Glass Seed Beads. Finished piece was custom framed.

Skill Level
****Challenging

Stitch Count
71 wide x 133 high

Approximate Design Size
11-count 6⅜" x 12"
14-count 5" x 9½"
16-count 4⅜" x 8¼"
18-count 4" x 7⅜"
22-count 3¼" x 6"
28-count over two threads 5" x 9½"

Instructions
1. Stitch design is in band order beginning 3 inches from one short end of fabric, stitching over two threads and using one or two strands floss or one strand braid or ombré as

indicated on key for Cross-Stitch. Use one strand of braid, cord or floss as indicated on key for Backstitch, Straight Stitch and Satin Stitch. Use one strand floss or braid for Lazy-Daisy Stitch. Couch (see illustration) laid thread using one strand cord as indicated on key. Use one strand coordinating silk floss for securing beads (see illustration on page 136). Use one strand braid and one strand ombré for Rice Stitch (see illustration). Use one strand braid for Four-Sided Stitch (see illustration). Use one strand floss and one strand ombré for Whipped Running Stitch (see illustration). ❖

Whipped Running Stitch

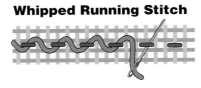

Lazy Daisy Stitch

Satin Stitch

Rice Stitch

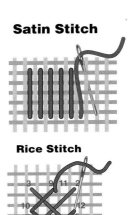

Four-sided Stitch

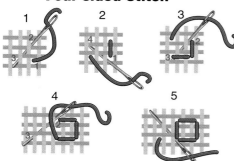

Work from right to left and stitch over four threads in each direction. (1) To start, come up at 1, go in at 2, exit at 3. (2) Go in at 1 and come up at 4. (3) Go in a 2, exit at 3. (4) Finally go in at 2, exit at 3 (last bar of first Four-sided Stitch forms first bar of second stitch). (5) Repeat steps 1-4 until row is completed. Pull each stitch tight.

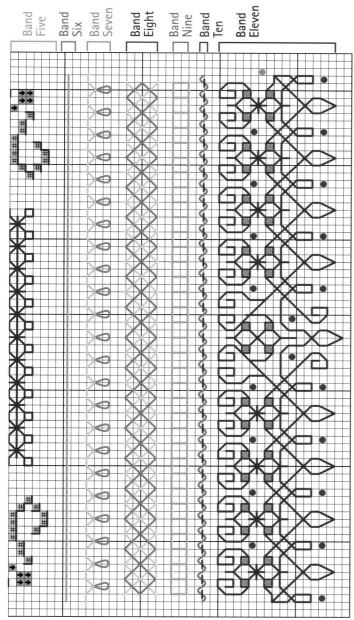

KREINIK

BAND ONE
| 6123 | ◻ | Light dusty lavender Silk Mori Cross-Stitch (1x) |
| 6123 | ▬ | Light dusty lavender Silk Mori Backstitch (1x) |

BAND TWO
| 225 | ▭ | Slate #8 Fine Braid (2x) and 001 silver #12 Tapestry Braid (1x) Laid Thread with 225 slate Cord (1x) Couching Thread |

BAND THREE
| 032 | ☐ | Pearl #4 Very Fine Braid Four-Sided Stitch (1x) |

BAND FOUR
| 1600 | ▬ | Misty lavender Ombré Backstitch (1x) |
| 6123 | ▭ | Light dusty lavender Silk Serica Backstitch (1x) |

BAND FIVE

CROSS-STITCH (1X)
001	◆◆	Silver Tapestry Braid
225	⊞	Slate #8 Fine Braid
1223	▼	Passion plum #8 Fine Braid
1600	−	Misty lavender Ombré
6123	V	Light dusty lavender Silk Mori

BACKSTITCH (1X)
001	▬	Silver Cord
032	▬	Pearl #4 Very Fine Braid
225	▬	Slate #8 Fine Braid Backstitch (1x)
225	▬	Slate Cord (1x)
6123	▬	Light dusty lavender Silk Serica Satin Stitch (1x)

OTHER STITCHES
001	▬	Silver Tapestry Braid (1x) Laid Thread with 001 silver Cord (1x) Couching Thread
225	▭	Slate #8 Fine Braid Laid Thread with 225 slate Cord Couching Thread
1092	▬	Lightest wood violet Silk Serica (1x) Laid Thread with 1092 lightest wood violet Silk Mori (1x) Couching Thread
032	⟋	Pearl #4 Very Fine Braid Lazy-Daisy Stitch (1X)
1092	▬	Lightest wood violet Silk Serica Satin Stitch (1x)
6123	▭	Light dusty lavender Silk Serica Satin Stitch (1x)

BEAD
| 00161 | ● | Crystal Mill Hill Seed Bead |

BAND SIX
| 1223 | ▬ | Passion plum #8 Fine Braid (2x) and 032 pearl #4 Very Fine Braid (1x) Laid Thread with 001 Silver Cord (1X) Couching Thread |

BAND SEVEN
| 6123 | ≈ | Light dusty lavender Silk Serica Backstitch (1x) |
| 6123 | ◊ | Light dusty lavender Silk Serica Lazy-Daisy Stitch (1x) |

BAND EIGHT
| 1223 | ▭ | Passion plum #8 Fine Braid Rice Stitch (first half) (1x) |
| 1600 | ▬ | Misty lavender Ombré Rice Stitch (second half) (1x) |

BAND NINE
| 032 | ☐ | Pearl #4 Very Fine Braid Four-Sided Stitch (1x) |

BAND TEN
| 225 | ⟿ | Slate #8 Fine Braid Running Stitch (1x) |
| 1600 | | Misty lavender Whipped (1x) for Running Whipped Stitch |

BAND ELEVEN
225	▬	Slate Cord Backstitch (1x)
00161	●	Crystal Mill Hill Seed Bead
00081	●	Jet Mill Hill Seed Bead

Couching Stitch

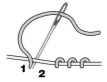

Happiness & Simplicity Mini Samplers

Designs by Catherine Bussi

These delicate framed pieces inspire us all to maintain a cheerful attitude.

Materials
- Antique white 18-count Aida:
  10 x 10 inches (each sampler)

"Happiness & Simplicity Mini Samplers" were stitched on white 18-count Aida by Zweigart using DMC floss. Finished pieces were custom framed.

Skill Level
**Average

Happiness Stitch Count
73 wide x 54 high

Approximate Design Size
11-count 6⅝" x 5"

14-count 5¼" x 3⅞"
16-count 4½" x 3⅜"
18-count 4" x 3"
22-count 3¼" x 2½"

Simplicity Stitch Count
76 wide x 58 high

Approximate Design Size
11-count 7" x 5¼"
14-count 5⅜" x 4"
16-count 4¾" x 3⅝"
18-count 4¼" x 3¼"
22-count 3½" x 2⅝"

Instructions
1. Center and stitch design using one strand floss for Cross-Stitch, Quarter Cross-Stitch, French Knot and Backstitch. ❖

Happiness

CROSS-STITCH (1X)

ANCHOR	DMC	COLORS	
2	·	White	White
387	I	Ecru	Ecru
120	^	159	Light gray blue
121	#	160	Medium gray blue
342	♡	211	Light lavender
118	/	340	Medium blue violet
117	••	341	Light blue violet
261	0	368	Light pistachio green
877	⊠	502	Blue green
876	:	503	Medium blue green
301	+	744	Pale yellow
300	o	745	Light pale yellow
271	−	819	Light baby pink
378	⅃	841	Light beige brown
1020	⌐	3713	Very light salmon
25	=	3716	Very light dusty rose
75	✿	3733	Dusty rose
120	::	3747	Very light blue violet
213	⌘	3817	Light celadon green
275	~	3823	Ultra pale yellow
869	Y	3836	Light grape
1002	<	3854	Medium autumn gold

QUARTER CROSS-STITCH (1X)

ANCHOR	DMC	COLORS	
302	✳	743	Medium yellow
360	♦	839	Dark beige brown

BACKSTITCH (1X)

ANCHOR	DMC	COLORS
121	160	Medium gray blue* (Simplicity: border)
122	161	Gray blue (Simplicity: birds, blue flowers; Happiness: blue flowers)
215	320	Medium pistachio green (Simplicity: yellow and blue flower stems; Happiness: blue flower stems)
118	340	Medium blue violet* (Simplicity: butterfly)
877	502	Blue green* (Simplicity: pink flower stems; Happiness: border)
360	839	Dark beige brown* (Simplicity: bee)
379	840	Medium beige brown (Simplicity: birdhouse pole, birdhouse opening; Happiness: butterflies)
871	3041	Medium antique violet (Happiness: violet flowers)
76	3731	Very dark dusty rose (Happiness: lettering)

BACKSTITCH (1X)

ANCHOR	DMC	COLORS
75	3733	Dusty rose* (Simplicity: birdhouse, small hearts, pink flowers; Happiness: hearts, pink flowers)
831	3782	Light mocha brown (Simplicity: fence)
216	3815	Dark celadon green (Simplicity: lettering; Happiness: stems above large heart)
1002	3854	Medium autumn gold* (Simplicity: birds' beaks and feet, yellow flowers)

FRENCH KNOT (1X)

ANCHOR	DMC	COLORS
121	●	160	Medium gray blue*

(Simplicity: birds' eyes, tiny flowers)

| 76 | ● | 3731 | Very dark dusty rose* |

(Happiness: dot above "i")

Duplicate color

Simplicity

Bold Blooms

Designs by Kathy Wirth

Place this trio of brightly colored blossoms wherever you need an unexpected punch of color.

Materials
For each
- Antique white 28-count Jobelan: 13 x 17 inches
- ¼-inch white foam board: 6 x 10 inches
  11 x 15 inches
- Coordinating fabric: 15 x 18 inches
  19 x 23 inches
- 1 yard ¼-inch white twisted satin cord
- Fabric adhesive
- Hanging hardware

"Bold Blooms" were stitched on antique white 28-count Jobelan by Wichelt Imports Inc. using Anchor floss.

Skill Level
**Average

Tulip Stitch Count
71 wide x 126 high

Approximate Design Size
11-count 6½" x 11½"
14-count 5" x 9"
16-count 4½" x 7⅞"
18-count 4" x 7"
22-count 3¼" x 5¾"
28-count over two threads 5" x 9"

Rose Stitch Count
77 wide x 125 high

Approximate Design Size
11-count 6½" x 11⅜"
14-count 5" x 9"
16-count 4½" x 7⅞"
18-count 4" x 7"

22-count 3¼" x 5¾"
28-count over two threads 5" x 9"

Sunflower Stitch Count
77 wide x 130 high

Approximate Design Size
11-count 7" x 11⅞"
14-count 5½" x 9¼"
16-count 4⅞" x 8⅛"
18-count 4¼ x 7¼"
22-count 3½" x 6"
28-count over two threads 5½" x 9¼"

Instructions
Note: Because there is no DMC equivalent to Anchor colors 101 and 102, DMC 550 is listed twice in the Tulip color key. The two Anchor shades are very similar, and if you decide to stitch with DMC floss you should not notice a significant difference in the finished piece.

1. Center and stitch design on Jobelan, stitching over two threads using three strands floss for Cross-Stitch and two strands floss for Backstitch.

Finishing
1. Center stitched piece on smaller piece of foam board, wrapping excess around board and mitering corners. Glue excess on back of board with fabric adhesive.

2. In same manner, cover larger piece of foam board with 19 x 23-inch piece of coordinating fabric. Turn under raw edges of 15 x 18-inch piece of coordinating fabric to fit back of foam board; glue or stitch in place.

3. Glue smaller board to center front of larger board. Use fabric adhesive to attach cord around edge of stitched board. Attach hanging hardware to back. ❖

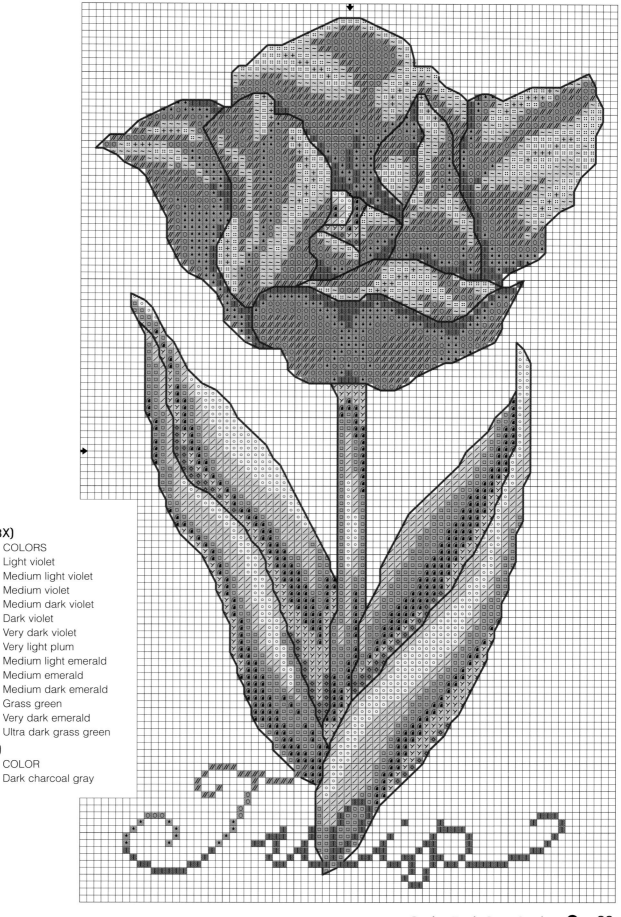

TULIP
CROSS-STITCH (3X)

DMC		ANCHOR	COLORS
3836	⋮⋮	96	Light violet
3608	~	97	Medium light violet
553	//	98	Medium violet
552	◎	100	Medium dark violet
550	♦	101	Dark violet
550	‖	102	Very dark violet
3609	+	103	Very light plum
702	╱	226	Medium light emerald
701	▫	227	Medium emerald
700	◪	228	Medium dark emerald
989	○	241	Grass green
699	Y	923	Very dark emerald
895	✿	1044	Ultra dark grass green

BACKSTITCH (2X)

DMC		ANCHOR	COLOR
3799	—	236	Dark charcoal gray

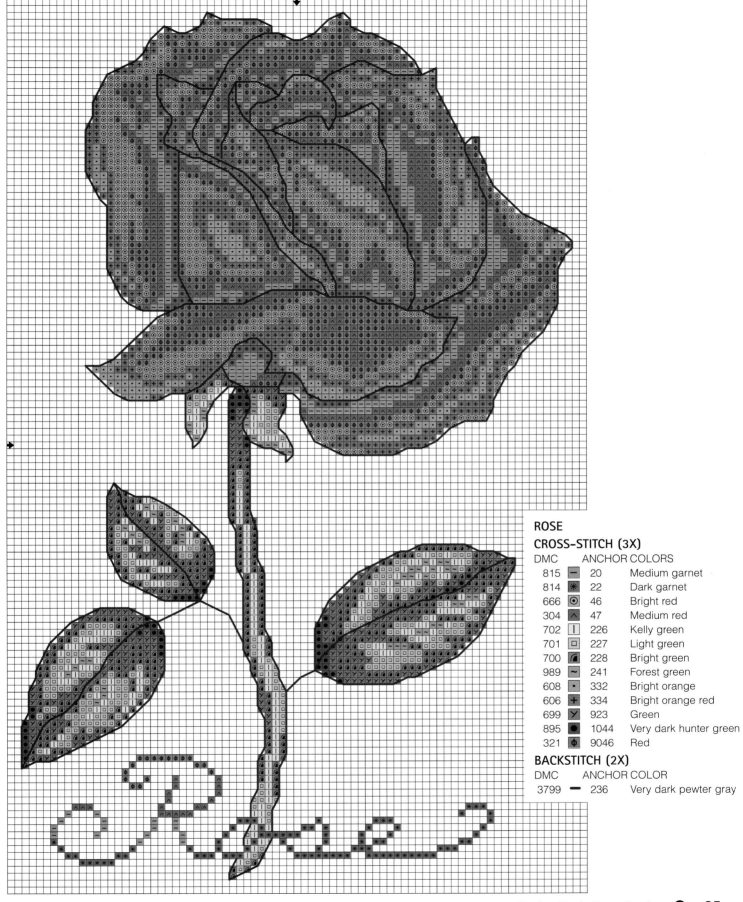

ROSE

CROSS-STITCH (3X)

DMC		ANCHOR	COLORS
815	▬	20	Medium garnet
814	✳	22	Dark garnet
666	⊙	46	Bright red
304	⋀	47	Medium red
702	▏	226	Kelly green
701	▢	227	Light green
700	◪	228	Bright green
989	~	241	Forest green
608	·	332	Bright orange
606	✚	334	Bright orange red
699	⋎	923	Green
895	●	1044	Very dark hunter green
321	φ	9046	Red

BACKSTITCH (2X)

DMC		ANCHOR	COLOR
3799	▬	236	Very dark pewter gray

SUNFLOWER
CROSS-STITCH (3X)

DMC		ANCHOR	COLORS
702	~	226	Kelly green
701			227	Light green
700	◢	228	Bright green
989	○	241	Forest green
727	∷	295	Very light topaz
444	+	297	Dark lemon
972	⊙	298	Deep canary
3852	//	306	Very dark straw
783	−	307	Medium topaz
782	☆	308	Dark topaz
781	◕	309	Very dark topaz
780	∧	310	Ultra very dark topaz
898	✖	360	Very dark coffee brown
938	⌐	381	Ultra dark coffee brown
699	✕	923	Green
895	▣	1044	Very dark hunter green

BACKSTITCH (2X)

DMC		ANCHOR	COLOR
3799	−	236	Very dark pewter gray

Garden Creatures

Design by Christine A. Hendricks

Bugs, bugs, bugs everywhere—but not to worry! They're friendly and cute and have come to live happily in your garden!

Materials

- White 14-count Aida (for Pillow) 13 x 16 inches
- White 14-mesh perforated plastic canvas (for plant poke)
- 10-count Waste Canvas (for Jeans)
- Graph paper
- Colored pencils or markers
- Jeans
- Bamboo skewer
- 1½ yards desired trim
- ½ yard fabric
- Polyester fiberfill
- Craft glue or glue gun

"Garden Creatures" was stitched on Aida by Wichelt Imports Inc., using DMC® floss.

Skill Level

**Average

Stitch Count

90 wide x 120 high

Approximate Design Size

11-count 11" x 8¼"
14-count 8⅝" x 6½"
16-count 7½" x 5⅝"
18-count 6¾" x 5"
22-count 5½" x 4⅛"

Instructions

1. For pillow front, center and stitch design on Aida, using two strands floss for Cross-Stitch and one strand floss for Backstitch and French Knot. Trim design 1 inch from stitched area. From fabric, cut one same as design for back.

Baste trim around edges of design. With right sides together, sew pillow front and back together with ½-inch seams, leaving a small opening. Turn right sides out; fill with fiberfill. Sew opening closed.

Note: Choose desired motifs for jeans and plant poke, and chart onto graph paper for proper placement.

2. For Jeans, position and baste Waste Canvas onto jeans, following manufacturer's instructions. Center and stitch design of choice, using four strands floss for Cross-Stitch and two strands floss for Backstitch and French Knot. Remove Waste Canvas after stitching, following manufacturer's instructions.

3. For plant poke, center and stitch design of choice onto perforated plastic canvas, using three strands floss for Cross-Stitch and one strand floss for Backstitch and French Knot. Trim design one hole from stitched area. Glue skewer on back of design. ❖

CROSS-STITCH (2X)

ANCHOR		DMC	COLORS
289	★	307	Lemon
403	⬆	310	Black
978	6	322	Dark dark baby blue
119	a	333	Very dark blue violet
118	/	340	Medium blue violet
11	T	350	Medium coral
374	◄	420	Dark hazelnut brown
288	U	445	Light lemon
1039	⊥	518	Light wedgewood
1038	n	519	Sky blue
62	✳	603	Cranberry
55	C	604	Light cranberry
334	0	606	Bright orange red
46	Y	666	Bright red

CROSS-STITCH (2X)

ANCHOR		DMC	COLORS
238	8	703	Chartreuse
295	▷	726	Light topaz
1012	–	754	Light peach
257	V	905	Dark parrot green
255	Z	907	Light parrot green
2	4	White	White

BACKSTITCH (1X)

ANCHOR		DMC	COLOR
403	▬	310	Black*

FRENCH KNOT (1X)

ANCHOR		DMC	COLORS
403	●	310	Black*
2	●	White	White*

Duplicate color

In my garden you will find little creatures of every kind

Making Pillows

By Carol Zentgraf

It's fun and easy to showcase a cross-stitch design on a pillow. Whether you create a pillow the same size as the stitched design or add a border, options abound for finishing.

Materials
- Coordinating fabric for backing and optional border
- Bead fringe or piping
- Pillow form or polyester fiberfill
- Water-soluble marking pen
- Coordinating all-purpose thread
- Self-adhesive double-sided basting tape (optional)
- Zipper equal to pillow width (optional)

Pillow cover

1. Clean and block the cross-stitch design. Trim and finish the edges 1 inch from the stitched edges. Use the water-soluble marking pen to draw a straight line around the design following the fabric weave to ensure straight edges.

2. To add a fabric border, decide the finished border width you would like, then add 1 inch for seams. For side borders, measure one side of the stitched design and add 1 inch for seams. Cut two strips equal to this measurement. For top border and bottom border, measure the top or bottom edge, add twice the width of one side border strip width and add 1 inch for seams; cut two strips. Using ½-inch seams and with right sides together, sew the side borders to the stitched design. Press seams open. Repeat for the top and bottom borders.

3. For the pillow back, cut a fabric piece equal to the front.

4. For a pillow without borders, cut a fabric piece equal in size to the stitched design, adding 1 inch to the width and length for seams.

5. To prevent floppy corners that often result on larger pillows when a pillow form is used or it is stuffed too firmly, with right sides together, fold the back into fourths and pin edges together. Mark the distance halfway between the corner and the fold on the two raw edges. Make another mark ½ inch from the corner and draw a line to connect the three marks. Cut through all layers on the marked lines. Open the trimmed panel and use it as a guide to shape the front.

6. To add piping or beaded trim, pin or use basting tape to position the trim along the front edges with the raw edges toward the outside. Use a zipper foot to sew the piping or trim in place.

7. For a pillow cover with a zipper, follow the manufacturer's instructions and sew the zipper along the lower edge before sewing the front to the back. Sew the pillow front to the back with right sides together and using ½-inch seams. For pillows without a zipper, leave an opening for inserting the pillow form or fiberfill (see "Stuffing Savvy" below). Turn the pillow right sides out and press. Insert the pillow form or stuff with polyester fiberfill. Zip or sew the opening closed.

Stuffing Savvy

To stuff or use a pillow form—the choice is up to you. Premade pillow forms are available ranging from 12 inches to 30 inches square and in limited round and rectangular sizes. You can also make your own form in the size and shape of your choice. A pillow form is especially desirable if you want to remove the cover for cleaning or if you would like to switch covers using the same form. Stuffing with polyester fiberfill is suitable for any pillow size, and is often the easiest option for small pillows or those with an irregular shape. To make a pillow form, use cotton or cotton blend fabric. The form should be the same size as the finished pillow cover to prevent floppy edges.

1. For a rectangular or square pillow, add 1 inch to the width and the length measurements for seams; cut two pieces. For a round or irregular-shaped pillow, draw the pillow outline onto the fabric for the form; add ½ inch for seams to all edges and cut two pieces.

2. Using ½ inch for seams, sew with right sides together, leaving an opening for turning. Turn right sides out and press the opening seam allowances under.

3. Stuff the pillow form, filling the corners evenly with polyester fiberfill; then stuff the rest of the cover to the desired fullness. The firmer you stuff the pillow, the more rounded it will become. Stitched designs with words or letters will be easier to read if not stuffed too firmly. Sew the opening closed. ❖

My First Bible

Design by Patricia Martin

Stitch a personal bookmark to go with a treasured first Bible.

Materials
- White 14-count Aida: 5 x 10 inches
- Graph paper
- Colored pencils or markers

"My First Bible" was stitched with DMC floss.

Skill Level
*Easy

Stitch Count
30 wide x 88 high

Approximate Design Size
11-count 2¾" x 8"
14-count 2¼" x 6⅜"
16-count 1⅞" x 5½"
18-count 1¾" x 5"
22-count 1⅜" x 4"

Instructions
Note: Choose desired letters from Alphabet graph for name and chart onto graph paper for proper placement.

1. Center and stitch design using two strands floss for Cross-Stitch and Backstitch and French Knot of lettering. Use one strand floss for remaining Backstitch.

2. Cut to size and fringe edges. ❖

CROSS-STITCH (2X)

ANCHOR		DMC	COLORS
110	↑	208	Very dark lavender
108	∴	210	Medium lavender
403	∞	310	Black
288	−	445	Light lemon
208	‹	563	Light jade
390	∧	822	Light beige gray
68	L	3687	Mauve
49	H	3689	Light mauve
701	○	5282	Gold metallic

BACKSTITCH (1X)

ANCHOR	DMC	COLOR
403	— 310	Black*

BACKSTITCH (2X)

ANCHOR	DMC	COLOR
131	— 798	Dark delft blue*

FRENCH KNOT (2X)

ANCHOR	DMC	COLOR
131	● 798	Dark delft blue*

Duplicate color

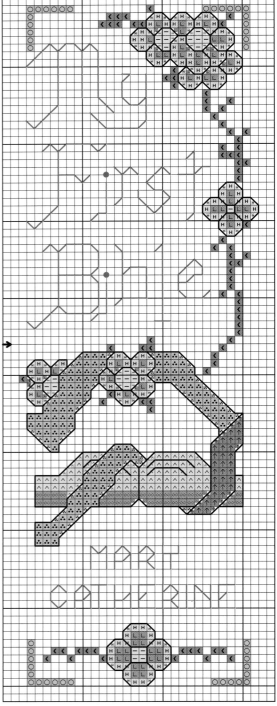

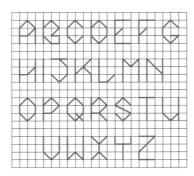

Lo, the Winter Is Over

Design by Gail Bussi

*As a new season arrives, welcome it with this bright
spring-fresh sampler from Bible verse Song of Solomon 2:11.*

Materials

- Antique white 32-count Belfast linen: 13 x 12 inches

"Lo, the Winter Is Over" was stitched on antique white 32-count Belfast Linen by Zweigart using DMC floss. Finished piece was custom framed.

Skill Level

***Intermediate

Stitch Count

107 wide x 89 high

Approximate Design Size

11-count 9¾" x 8⅛"
14-count 7¾" x 6⅜"
16-count 6¾" x 5⅝"
18-count 6" x 5"
22-count 4⅞" x 4⅛"
32-count over two threads 6¾" x 5⅝"

Instructions

1. Center and stitch design over two threads, using one or two strands floss as indicated on the color key for Cross-Stitch. Use one strand floss for Half Cross-Stitch, Backstitch, Lazy-Daisy Stitch and French Knot, wrapping twice. ❖

CROSS-STITCH (2X)

ANCHOR	DMC	COLORS
2	White	White
109	209	Dark lavender
342	211	Light lavender
215	320	Medium pistachio green
261	368	Light pistachio green
1043	369	Very light pistachio green
832	612	Light drab brown
361	738	Very light tan
1022	760	Salmon
1021	761	Light salmon
390	822	Light beige gray
1033	932	Light antique blue
243	988	Medium forest green
242	989	Forest green
842	3013	Light khaki green
903	3032	Medium mocha brown
262	3052	Medium green gray
264	3348	Light yellow green
260	3364	Pine green
1020	3713	Very light salmon
1032	3752	Very light antique blue
831	3782	Light mocha brown
393	3790	Ultra dark beige gray
275	3823	Ultra pale yellow
888	3828	Hazelnut brown
1002	3854	Medium autumn gold
301	3855	Light autumn gold

CROSS-STITCH (1X)

ANCHOR	DMC	COLORS
261	368	Light pistachio green*
264	3348	Light yellow green*
260	3364	Pine green*
1032	3752	Very light antique blue*

HALF CROSS-STITCH (1X)

ANCHOR	DMC	COLOR
2	White	White*

BACKSTITCH (1X)

ANCHOR	DMC	COLORS
401	413	Dark pewter gray
832	612	Light drab brown
244	987	Dark forest green
266	3347	Medium yellow green
393	3790	Ultra dark beige gray*
1002	3854	Medium autumn gold*

LAZY-DAISY STITCH (1X)

ANCHOR	DMC	COLOR
266	3347	Medium yellow green*

FRENCH KNOT (1X)

ANCHOR	DMC	COLORS
109	209	Dark lavender*
1033	932	Light antique blue*
381	938	Ultra dark coffee brown
244	987	Dark forest green*
1023	3712	Medium salmon

*Duplicate color

Heart's Delight Pillow

Design by Gail Bussi

This little pillow makes a cherished reminder of how much you care for a friend!

CROSS-STITCH (2X)

ANCHOR		DMC	COLORS
108	∞	210	Medium lavender
215	9	320	Medium pistachio green
118	✦✦	340	Medium blue violet
117	#	341	Light blue violet
261	$	368	Light pistachio green
1043	%	369	Very light pistachio green
1045	••	436	Tan
362	▣	437	Light tan
877	(	502	Blue green
301	)	744	Pale Yellow
300	✳	745	Light pale yellow
24	+	776	Medium pink
271	8	819	Light baby pink
52	↑	899	Medium rose
903	–	3032	Medium mocha brown
36	·	3326	Light rose
1050	5	3781	Dark mocha brown
831	:	3782	Light mocha brown
213	O	3813	Light blue green
215	1	3816	Medium celadon green
145	3	3839	Medium lavender blue
144	4	3840	Light lavender blue
2	7	White	White

BACKSTITCH (1X)

ANCHOR		DMC	COLORS
215	—	320	Medium pistachio green*
261	—	368	Light pistachio green*
52	—	899	Medium rose*
36	—	3326	Light rose*
260	—	3364	Pine green
1050	—	3781	Dark mocha brown*
215	—	3816	Celadon green*

RUNNING STITCH (1X)

ANCHOR		DMC	COLOR
52	—	899	Medium rose*

FRENCH KNOT (2X)

ANCHOR		DMC	COLORS
301	○	744	Pale yellow*
1050	●	3781	Dark mocha brown*

*Duplicate color

Materials

- White 32-count Lugana:
  13 x 11 inches
- Backing fabric
- 1-inch-wide gathered eyelet ruffle
- Contrasting piping
- Polyester fiberfill

"Heart's Delight Pillow" was stitched on white 32-count Lugana by Zweigart using DMC floss.

Skill Level
**Average

Stitch Count
110 wide x 80 wide

Approximate Design Size
11-count 10" x 7"

14-count 7⅞" x 5¾"
16-count 6⅞" x 5"
18-count 6" x 4⅜"
22-count 5" x 3⅝"
32-count over two threads 6⅞" x 5"

Instructions

1. Center and stitch design, stitching over two threads and using two strands floss for Cross-Stitch and French Knot, and one strand floss for Backstitch and Running Stitch.

Finishing

Note: Use ½-inch seam allowance.

1. For front, trim stitched piece to 1 inch from stitching. Cut backing fabric same as front.

2. Baste piping and eyelet ruffle to front. Sew backing and front right sides together, leaving an opening for turning.

3. Turn pillow right sides out; fill with fiberfill. Slipstitch opening closed. ❖

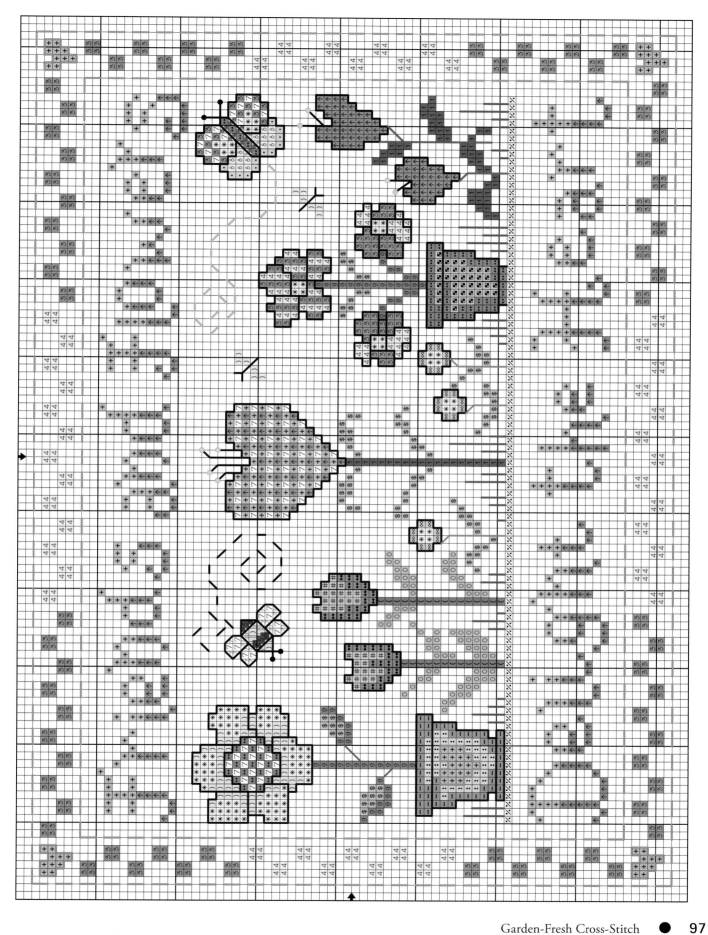

Love Is a Gift

Design by Ursula Michaels

Stitch as is for a beautiful anniversary gift, or customize with a date to create a special wedding gift.

Materials
- Bridal white 30-count Melinda: 14 x 14 inches

"Love Is a Gift" was stitched on bridal white 30-count Melinda by Wichelt Imports Inc. using floss from DMC. Finished piece was custom framed.

Skill Level
**Average

Stitch Count
120 wide x 120 high

Approximate Design Size
11-count 11" x 11"
14-count 8½" x 8½"
16-count 7½" x 7½"
18-count 6⅝" x 6⅝"
22-count 5½" x 5½"
30-count over two threads 8" x 8"

Instructions
1. Center and stitch design on 30-count Melinda, stitching over two threads using two strands floss for Cross-Stitch and all stitches in center area, and one strand floss for Backstitch. ❖

CROSS-STITCH (2X)

ANCHOR		DMC	COLORS
42	■	309	Dark rose
218	■	319	Very dark pistachio green
215	✳	320	Medium pistachio green
261	⬍	368	Light pistachio green
302	♡	743	Medium yellow
23	$	818	Baby pink
160	✔	827	Very light blue
52	◇	899	Medium rose
1011	╱	948	Very light peach
36	m	3326	Light rose
264	V	3348	Light yellow green
1020	⊠	3713	Very light salmon
1013	·	3778	Light terra cotta
305	−	3821	Straw
2	⌐	White	White

BACKSTITCH (1X)

ANCHOR		DMC	COLORS
59	—	326	Very dark rose
162	—	825	Dark blue
897	—	3857	Dark rosewood

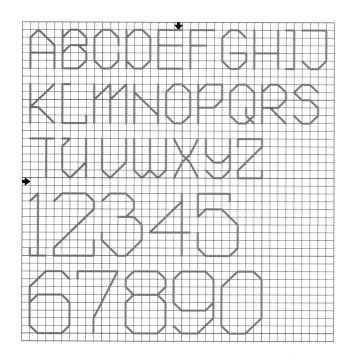

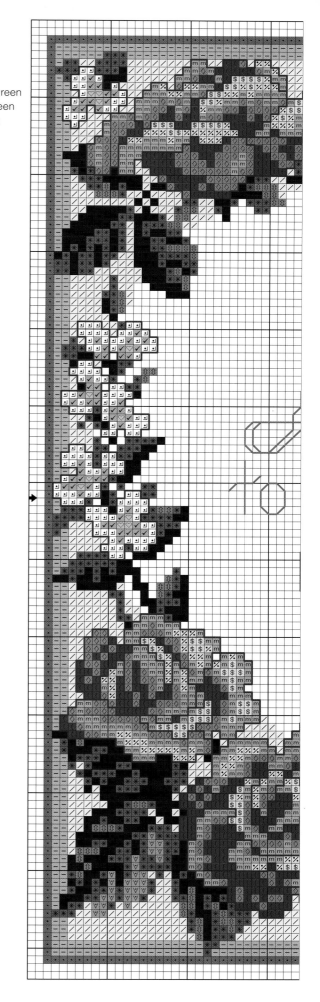

My Daughter, My Treasure

Design by Janice Lockhart

Stitched in soft shades of rose and sage green, and accented with coordinating seed and bugle beads, this treasure box will become a family heirloom to be passed down through generations to come.

Materials
- Cream 32-count pure Irish linen: 11 x 11 inches
- Mill Hill beads:
  tea rose #02004 seed
  royal plum #02012 seed
  dusty rose #72005 small bugle
- Square hinged-lid wooden box with 5 x 5-inch inside-mount design area

"My Daughter, My Treasure" was stitched on cream 32-count pure Irish linen by Charles Craft using DMC floss and Mill Hill seed beads and small bugle beads. Finished piece was inserted in Square Box #99001 Wood Stain by Sudberry House.

Skill Level
**Average

Stitch Count
76 wide x 76 high

Approximate Design Size
11-count 7" x 7"
14-count 5⅜" x 5⅜"
16-count 4¾" x 4¾"

18-count 4¼" x 4¼"
22-count 3½" x 3½"
32-count over two threads 4¾" x 4¾"

Instructions

1. Center and stitch design on linen using two strands floss for Cross-Stitch, and one strand floss for Backstitch.

2. Attach beads (see Bead Attachment illustration on page 136) as indicated on graph using two strands coordinating floss.

Finishing

1. Insert stitched piece in box following manufacturer's directions. ❖

CROSS-STITCH (2X)

ANCHOR		DMC	COLORS
860	◣	522	Fern green
859	+	523	Light fern green
858	∷	524	Very light fern green
301	☆	744	Pale yellow
300	~	745	Light pale yellow
24	☑	776	Medium pink
23	/	818	Baby pink
52	△	899	Medium rose
681	−	3051	Dark green gray
59	(	3350	Ultra dark dusty rose
25	◉	3716	Very light dusty rose
275	♡	3823	Ultra pale yellow

BACKSTITCH (1X)

ANCHOR		DMC	COLORS
681	—	3051	Dark green gray* (leaves)
59	—	3350	Ultra dark dusty rose* (flowers, lettering)

ATTACH BEAD

MILL HILL SEED BEAD

| 02004 | ● | Tea rose, with #3716 very light dusty rose* (2X) |
| 02012 | ● | Royal plum, with #3350 ultra dark dusty rose* (2X) |

MILL HILL SMALL BUGLE BEAD

| 72005 | — | Dusty rose, with #3716 very light dusty rose* (2X) |

Duplicate color

Floral Teacup

Design by June Fiechter

This piece is proof that easy stitching can still have a detailed look!

Materials
- Daffodil 20-count Laguna:
  12 x 13 inches

"Floral Teacup" was stitched on daffodil 20-count Laguna by Zweigart using DMC floss.

Skill Level
*Easy

Stitch Count
60 wide x 66 high

Approximate Design Size
11-count 5½" x 6"
14-count 4¼" x 4¾"
16-count 3¾" x 4⅛"
18-count 3⅜" x 3⅝"
22-count 2¾" x 3"

Instructions
1. Center and stitch design over two threads using four strands floss for Cross-Stitch and two strands floss for Backstitch and French Knot. ❖

CROSS-STITCH (4X)

ANCHOR		DMC	COLORS
2	·	White	White
267	✳	469	Avocado green
859	○	523	Light fern green
63	#	602	Medium cranberry
238	∧	703	Chartreuse
304	✕	741	Medium tangerine
259	+	772	Very light yellow green
941	◇	792	Dark cornflower blue
130	▣	809	Delft blue
45	✿	814	Dark garnet

CROSS-STITCH (4X)

ANCHOR		DMC	COLORS
1033	~	932	Light antique blue
50	╱	957	Pale geranium
297	=	973	Bright canary
264	◣	3348	Light yellow green
49	∷	3689	Light mauve
120	ဢ	3747	Very light blue violet
1037	⅄	3756	Ultra very light baby blue

BACKSTITCH (2X)

ANCHOR		DMC	COLORS
267	—	469	Avocado green* (stems, leaves)
130	—	809	Delft blue* (blue flowers)
45	—	814	Dark garnet* (pink flowers)
134	—	820	Very dark royal blue (lettering, teacup)

FRENCH KNOT (2X)

ANCHOR		DMC	COLOR
134	●	820	Very dark royal blue*

Duplicate color

Patchwork Welcome

Design by Lois Winston

Welcome friends and loved ones with traditional quilt-block motifs stitched in country colors. Country shades of blue, peach, green and lavender form the basis of a traditional welcome sign. Hang it in a foyer where it will warmly greet your guests!

Materials
• Antique white 14-count Aida:
  17 x 17 inches

"Patchwork Welcome" was stitched on antique white 14-count Aida by Wichelt using DMC floss. Finished piece was custom framed.

Skill Level
**Average

Stitch Count
153 wide x 153 high

Approximate Design Size
11-count 14" x 14"
14-count 11" x 11"
16-count 9½" x 9½"
18-count 8½" x 8½"
22-count 7" x 7"

Instructions
1. Center and stitch design on 14-count Aida, using three strands floss for Cross-Stitch. ❖

CROSS-STITCH (3X)

ANCHOR		DMC	COLORS
897	⊥	221	Very dark shell pink
893	⊡	224	Very light shell pink
683	‖	500	Very dark blue green
877	✳	502	Blue green
1042	╱	504	Very light blue green
1038	✕	519	Sky blue
359	╲	801	Dark coffee brown
1027	♡	3722	Medium shell pink
161	⊞	3760	Medium wedgewood
213	~	3813	Light blue green
888	O	3828	Hazlenut brown
873	V	3834	Dark grape
872	A	3835	Medium grape
869	✤	3836	Light grape
164	●	3842	Dark wedgewood

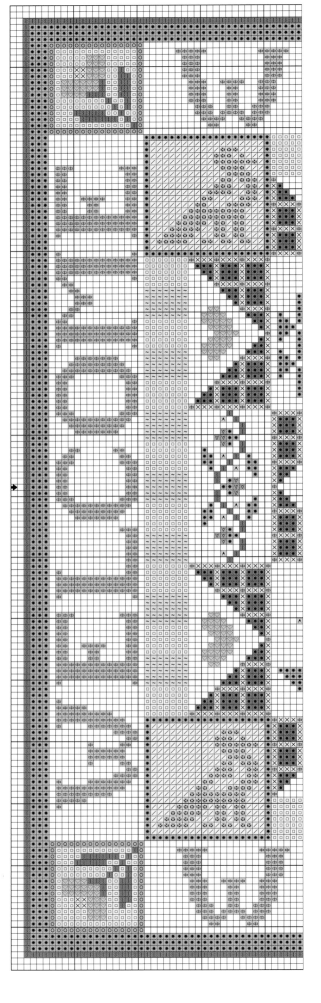

If Friends Were Flowers

Design by Robin Kingsley

A friendly "scentiment" will remind a special someone that they're in your heart at all times!

Materials

- Daffodil 22-count Softana:
  12 x 15 inches
- Mill Hill #00161 crystal seed beads
- Brass heart charm

"If Friends Were Flowers" was stitched on daffodil 22-count Softana fabric by Zweigart using DMC floss and Mill Hill beads from Gay Bowles Sales Inc. Finished piece was custom framed.

Skill Level
*Easy

Stitch Count
62 wide x 92 high

Approximate Design Size

11-count 5¾" x 8⅜"
14-count 4½" x 6½"
16-count 4" x 5¾"
18-count 3½" x 5"
22-count 2⅞" x 4⅛"
22-count over two threads 5¾" x 8⅜"

Instructions

1. Center and stitch design on Softana, stitching over two threads using four strands floss for Cross-Stitch, and two strands floss for Lazy-Daisy Stitch, Backstitch and French Knot.

2. Attach beads (see Bead Attachment illustration on page 136) and heart charm as indicated on graph, using one strand coordinating floss. ❖

CROSS-STITCH (4X)

ANCHOR	DMC	COLORS
979	312	Very dark baby blue
9046	321	Red
977	334	Medium baby blue
358	433	Medium brown
295	726	Light topaz
307	783	Medium topaz
257	905	Dark parrot green
256	906	Medium parrot green
255	907	Light parrot green
381	938	Ultra dark coffee brown
292	3078	Very light golden yellow
129	3325	Light baby blue
68	3687	Mauve
66	3688	Medium mauve
49	3689	Light mauve
869	3836	Light grape

LAZY-DAISY STITCH (2X)

ANCHOR	DMC	COLOR
381	938	Ultra dark coffee brown*

BACKSTITCH (2X)

ANCHOR	DMC	COLORS
256	906	Medium parrot green*
381	938	Ultra dark coffee brown*

FRENCH KNOT (2X)

ANCHOR	DMC	COLOR
381	938	Ultra dark coffee brown*

ATTACH BEAD

MILL HILL SEED BEAD
00161		Crystal

ATTACH CHARM

	Heart charm

*Duplicate color

Lazy-Daisy Stitch

Country Sentiments Dish Towels

Designs by Robin Kingsley

Stitch these simple thoughts on towels, as shown here, or stitch them to frame as daily reminders of a simple life!

Materials
- 2 ecru huck towels with 14-count 5 x 7-inch display area

"Country Sentiments Dish Towels" were stitched on ecru Showcase Towels HF-6500-6750 from Charles Craft Inc. using floss from DMC.

Skill Level
**Average

Stitch Count
52 wide x 74 high

Approximate Design Size
11-count 4¾" x 6¾"
14-count 3¾" x 5¼"
16-count 3¼" x 4⅝"
18-count 2⅞" x 4"
22-count 2⅜" x 3⅜"

Instructions
1. Center and stitch design in display area of towel using three strands floss for Cross-Stitch and one strand floss for Lazy-Daisy Stitch. Use two strands floss for Backstitch on letters and one strand floss for remaining Backstitch. Use two strands floss for French Knot on lettering; use one strand floss for remaining French Knots. ❖

LIVE SIMPLY LIVE WELL
CROSS-STITCH (3X)

ANCHOR		DMC	COLORS
978	V	322	Dark baby blue
11	–	350	Medium coral
9	♡	352	Light coral
253	∧	472	Ultra light avocado green
891	X	676	Light old gold
886	=	677	Very light old gold
890	◩	729	Medium old gold
13	::	817	Very dark coral red
381	▩	938	Ultra dark coffee brown
246	✳	986	Very dark forest green
244	+	987	Dark forest green
242	△	989	Forest green
140	□	3755	Baby blue
1015	Y	3777	Very dark terra cotta
295	╱	3822	Light straw
307	O	3852	Very dark straw

LAZY-DAISY STITCH (1X)

ANCHOR		DMC	COLOR
381	━	938	Ultra dark coffee brown*

BACKSTITCH (2X)

ANCHOR		DMC	COLOR
381	—	938	Ultra dark coffee brown*

BACKSTITCH (1X)

ANCHOR		DMC	COLORS
978	—	322	Dark baby blue*
381	—	938	Ultra dark coffee brown*
246	—	986	Very dark forest green*

FRENCH KNOT (2X)

ANCHOR		DMC	COLOR
381	●	938	Ultra dark coffee brown*

FRENCH KNOT (1X)

ANCHOR		DMC	COLOR
381	●	938	Ultra dark coffee brown*

*Duplicate color

AN APPLE A DAY

CROSS-STITCH (3X)

ANCHOR	DMC	COLORS
11	350	Medium coral
9	352	Light coral
891	676	Light old gold
926	712	Cream
305	725	Medium light topaz
13	817	Very dark coral red
381	938	Ultra dark coffee brown
246	986	Very dark forest green
244	987	Dark forest green
242	989	Forest green
1015	3777	Very dark terra cotta

LAZY-DAISY STITCH (1X)

ANCHOR	DMC	COLOR
381	938	Ultra dark coffee brown*

BACKSTITCH (2X)

ANCHOR	DMC	COLOR
381	938	Ultra dark coffee brown*

BACKSTITCH (1X)

ANCHOR	DMC	COLORS
381	938	Ultra dark coffee brown*
246	986	Very dark forest green*

FRENCH KNOT (2X)

ANCHOR	DMC	COLOR
381	938	Ultra dark coffee brown*

FRENCH KNOT (1X)

ANCHOR	DMC	COLOR
381	938	Ultra dark coffee brown*

*Duplicate color

Lazy-Daisy Stitch

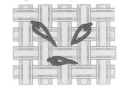

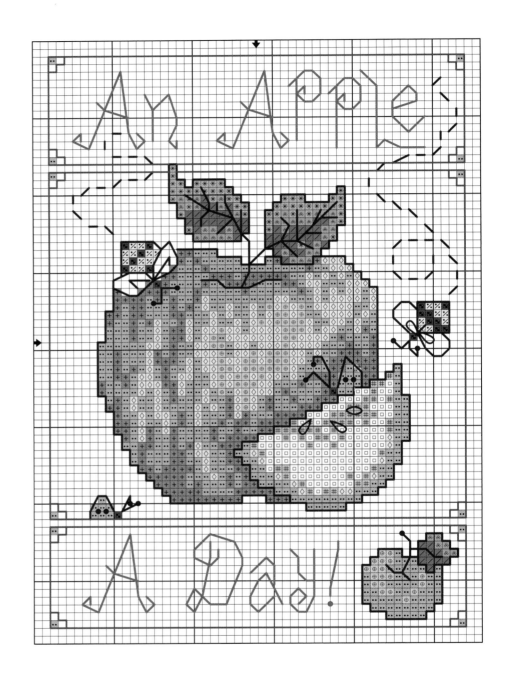

Garden Guardian

Design by Roberta Rankin

Let this garden angel keep watch over your new sprouts.

CROSS-STITCH (2X)

ANCHOR		DMC	COLORS
109	⊄	209	Dark lavender
108	⊗	210	Medium lavender
117	$	341	Light blue violet
8	⌶	353	Peach
5975	◪	356	Medium terra cotta
1045	✳	436	Tan
62	◁	603	Cranberry
55	✕	604	Light cranberry
50	⦅	605	Very light cranberry
830	⌗	644	Medium beige brown
886	◇	677	Very light old gold
295	⌒e	726	Light topaz
293	T	727	Very light topaz
361	⊘	738	Very light tan
275	+	746	Off white
882	⌟	758	Very light terra cotta
259	L	772	Very light yellow green
144	4	800	Pale delft blue
130	C	809	Delft blue
378	✿	841	Light beige brown
368	?	842	Very light beige brown
52	↑	899	Medium rose
1011	⊘	948	Very light peach
203	=	954	Nile green
73	⌶	963	Ultra very light dusty rose
847	H	3072	Very light beaver gray

CROSS-STITCH (2X)

ANCHOR		DMC	COLORS
292	V	3078	Very light golden yellow
129	7	3325	Light baby blue
266	✚	3347	Medium yellow green
264	S	3348	Light yellow green
35	☐	3705	Dark melon
928	n	3811	Very light turquoise
295	♡	3822	Dark straw
1003	⇨	3853	Dark autumn gold
1002	⚓	3854	Medium autumn gold
2	·	White	White

BACKSTITCH (2X)

ANCHOR		DMC	COLOR
129	—	3325	Light baby blue*

BACKSTITCH (1X)

ANCHOR		DMC	COLORS
361	—	738	Very light tan*
255	—	907	Light parrot green
1001	—	976	Medium golden brown
847	—	3072	Very light beaver gray
129	—	3325	Light baby blue*
35	—	3705	Dark melon*

FRENCH KNOT (1X)

ANCHOR		DMC	COLORS
129	●	3325	Light baby blue*
35	●	3705	Dark melon*

*Duplicate color

Materials
- White 14-count Aida:
  13 x 15 inches

"Garden Guardian" was stitched using DMS floss. Finished design was custom framed.

Skill Level
**Average

Stitch Count
120 wide x 89 high

Approximate Design Size
11-count 11" x 8⅛"
14-count 8⅝" x 6⅜"
16-count 7½" x 5⅝"

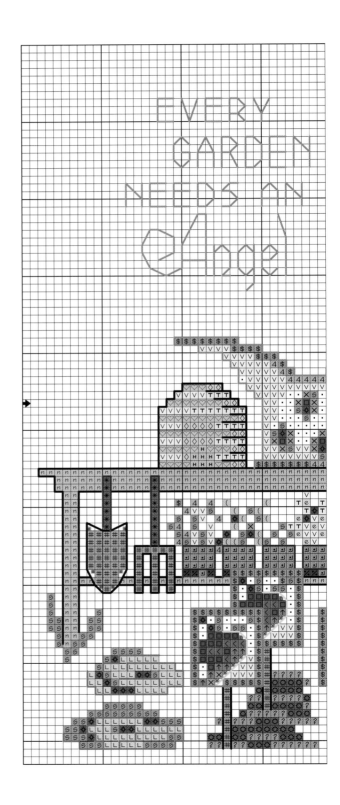

18-count 6¾" x 5"
22-count 5½" x 4⅛"

Instructions

1. Center and stitch design, using two
strands floss for Cross-Stitch and Backstitch
of lettering. Use one strand floss for
remaining Backstitch and French Knot. ❖

Russian Khokhloma–Berries

Design by Barbara Sestok

Khokhloma is a Russian folk-art painting technique. The colorful floral and fruit motifs translate quite well into cross-stitch!

Materials

- Light sand 28-count Cashel linen: 11 x 11 inches
- 8½ x 9½-inch wooden collector's cabinet with 3½ x 3½-inch design area

"Russian Khokhloma—Berries" was stitched on light sand 28-count Cashel linen by Zweigart using Anchor floss. Finished piece was inserted in Small Collector's Cabinet #35341 from Sudberry House.

Skill Level

**Average

Stitch Count

43 wide x 45 high

Approximate Design Size

11-count 3⅞" x 4"
14-count 3" x 3¼"
16-count 2½" x 2⅞"
18-count 2¼" x 2½"
22-count 1⅞" x 2"
28-count over two threads 3" x 3¼"

Instructions

1. Center and stitch design, stitching over two threads using three strands floss for Cross-Stitch, three strands or one strand floss for Backstitch, and two strands floss for Lazy-Daisy Stitch. Use number of strands and wraps for French Knot as indicated on color key.

Finishing

1. Insert stitched piece in cabinet following manufacturer's directions. ❖

CROSS-STITCH (3X)

DMC		ANCHOR	COLORS
321	−	47	Red
3078	◸	292	Very light golden yellow
3852	⠿	306	Very dark straw
3012	◿	843	Medium khaki green

LAZY-DAISY STITCH (2X)

DMC		ANCHOR	COLOR
3012	−	843	Medium khaki green*

BACKSTITCH (3X)

DMC		ANCHOR	COLOR
3852	−	306	Very dark straw* (curlicues)

BACKSTITCH (1X)

DMC		ANCHOR	COLORS
321	−	47	Red*
3852	−	306	Very dark straw* (leaves)
310	−	403	Black

FRENCH KNOT (4X, WRAP ONCE)

DMC		ANCHOR	COLOR
3852	●	306	Very dark straw*

FRENCH KNOT (3X, WRAP TWICE)

DMC		ANCHOR	COLORS
321	●	47	Red*
3078	●	292	Very light golden yellow*

FRENCH KNOT (2X, WRAP ONCE)

DMC		ANCHOR	COLOR
310	●	403	Black*

Duplicate color

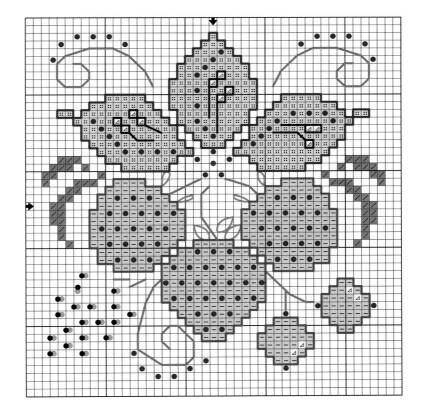

Lazy-Daisy Stitch

Patchwork Pumpkin Pin

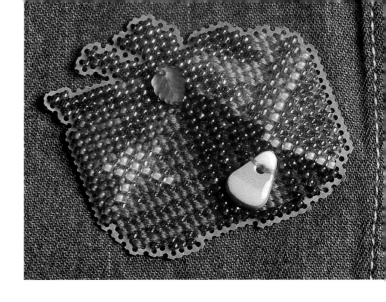

Design by Mill Hill

Beads and buttons add a bit of shine to a patchwork pumpkin that stitches up in no time at all!

Materials
- Antique brown 14-count perforated paper
- Mill Hill glass seed and petite beads as listed in color key
- Mill Hill Treasure olive medium leaf button #12144
- Mill Hill petite candy corn button #86344
- Pin back
- Permanent adhesive

"Patchwork Pumpkin Pin" was stitched on Mill Hill antique brown 14-count perforated paper using floss from DMC and Mill Hill beads and buttons.

Skill Level
**Average

Stitch Count
30 wide x 28 high

Approximate Design Size
11-count 2¾" x 2½"
14-count 2⅛" x 2"
16-count 1⅞" x 1¾"
18-count 1⅝" x 1½"
22-count 1⅜" x 1¼"

Instructions
1. Stitch design on perforated paper using two strands floss for Cross-Stitch and two strands floss for attaching beads and buttons (see Bead Attachment illustration on page 136).

Finishing
1. Trim perforated paper to one hole beyond stitching.

2. Glue pin back to back. ❖

CROSS-STITCH (2X)

ANCHOR	DMC		COLORS
324	ⓞ	721	Medium orange spice
333	◉	900	Dark burnt orange
111	⁞⁞	3837	Ultra dark lavender

ATTACH BEAD

MILL HILL SEED		COLORS
00167	●	Christmas green, attach with 266/3347 medium yellow green (2X)
02033	●	Brilliant orange, attach with 324/721 medium orange spice* (2X)
02042	●	Matte pumpkin, attach with 324/721 medium orange spice* (2X)
02047	●	Soft willow, attach with 266/3347 medium yellow green* (2X)
02086	●	Purple electra, attach with 111/3837 ultra dark lavender* (2X)
62041	○	Frosted buttercup, attach with 300/745 light pale yellow (2X)

MILL HILL PETITE		COLORS
42011	○	Victorian gold, attach with 300/745 light pale yellow* (2X)
42031	○	Citron, attach with 266/3347 medium yellow green* (2X)
42033	●	Autumn flame, attach with 324/721 medium orange spice* (2X)

ATTACH BUTTON

MILL HILL TREASURE		
12144	●	Olive medium leaf, attach with 266/3347 medium yellow green* (2X)

MILL HILL BUTTON		
86344	●	Petite candy corn, attach with 324/721 medium orange spice* (2X)

Duplicate color

Kitchen Alphabet

Design by Lois Winston

Finish this stitched piece as a panel to attach to a canvas tote bag that's just right for carrying produce home from the market.

Materials
- Antique white 28-count Lugana: 15 x 21 inches
- 12 x 16-inch navy canvas tote bag

"Kitchen Alphabet" was stitched on antique white 28-count Lugana from Zweigart using floss from DMC.

Skill Level
**Average

Stitch Count
126 wide x 194 high

Approximate Design Size
11-count 11½" x 17⅝"
14-count 9" x 13⅞"
16-count 7⅞" x 12⅛"
18-count 7" x 10⅞"
22-count 5¾" x 8⅞"
28-count over two threads 9" x 13⅞"

Instructions
1. Center and stitch design on 28-count Lugana, stitching over two threads using two strands floss for Cross-Stitch, and one strand floss for Backstitch and French Knot.

Finishing
1. Trim stitched piece 1 inch from outside of border on all four sides. Turn raw edges under ¼ inch; turn under again ½ inch. Hand- or machine-stitch hem in place. ❖

CROSS-STITCH (2X)

ANCHOR		DMC	COLORS
109	✳	209	Dark lavender
403	▣	310	Black
148	·	311	Medium navy blue
9046	√	321	Red
978	+	322	Dark dark baby blue
100	◢	327	Dark violet
1025	○	347	Very dark salmon
11	△	350	Medium coral
358	⊟	433	Medium brown
1046	¶	435	Very light brown
362	⊘	437	Light tan
1005	‖	498	Dark red
900	♦	648	Light beaver grey
891	○	676	Light old gold
926	⊡	712	Cream
293	★	727	Very light topaz
890	~	729	Medium old gold
387	∞	739	Ultra very light tan
882	✕	758	Very light terra cotta
395	◣	801	Dark coffee brown
43	▽	815	Medium garnet
13	⌘	817	Very dark coral red
23	∷	818	Baby pink
379	▦	840	Medium beige brown
378	✛	841	Light beige brown
368	╱	842	Very light beige brown
1044	▬	895	Very dark hunter green
52	⋂	899	Medium rose
846	▦	3011	Dark khaki green
843	◗	3012	Medium khaki green
847	▢	3072	Very light beaver grey
36	✳	3326	Light rose
267	◎	3346	Hunter green
264	⊥	3348	Light yellow green
1023	▷	3712	Medium salmon
1013	☆	3778	Light terra cotta
275	⊞	3823	Ultra pale yellow
888	✿	3828	Hazelnut brown
341	⊞	3830	Terra cotta
111	✾	3837	Ultra dark lavender
1003	◨	3853	Dark autumn gold
1002	≪	3854	Medium autumn gold
301	▥	3855	Light autumn gold
1047	○	3856	Ultra very light mahogany
2	◖	3865	Winter white

BACKSTITCH (1X)

ANCHOR		DMC	COLOR
403	—	310	Black*

FRENCH KNOT (1X)

ANCHOR		DMC	COLOR
403	●	310	Black*

*Duplicate color

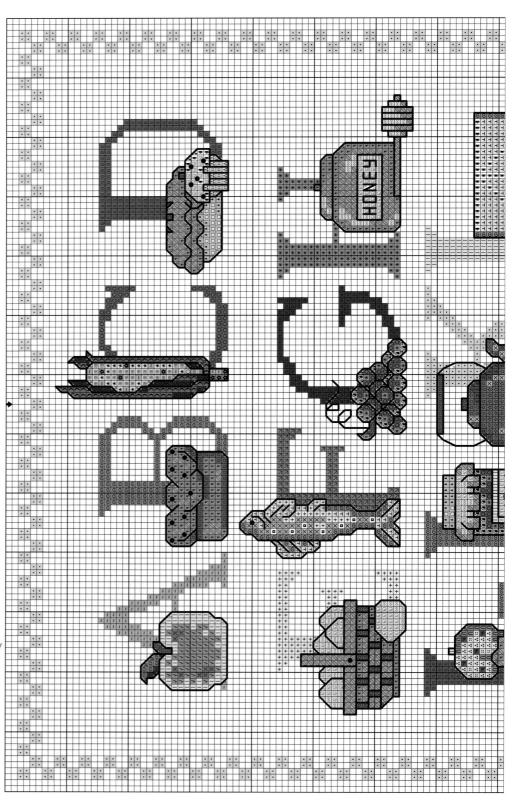

Canning-Jar Tags

Designs by Pamela Kellogg

Give two gifts in one—a jar of preserves from your garden and a canning-jar tag that can be used as a magnet after the goodies are gone!

Materials

- Ivory 14-count plastic canvas: 1 sheet
- 1 (10-inch) length each red, brown and purple 24-gauge craft wire by AMACO
- Needle-nose pliers

"Canning-Jar Tags" were stitched on ivory 14-count plastic canvas using DMC floss.

Skill Level

*Easy

Stitch Count

41 wide x 29 high

Approximate Design Size

11-count 3¾" x 2⅝"
14-count 3" x 2⅛"
16-count 2½" x 1⅞"
18-count 2¼" x 1⅝"
22-count 1⅞" x 1⅜"

Instructions

1. Stitch designs on plastic canvas using three strands floss for Cross-Stitch and two strands floss for Backstitch.

Finishing

1. Cut plastic canvas one hole beyond stitching.

2. Insert ends of wire through corner holes of each tag from back to front so that ends extend approximately 1 inch; use needle-nose pliers to coil ends to hold in place. ❖

Homemade With Love

HOMEMADE WITH LOVE
CROSS-STITCH (3X)

ANCHOR		DMC	COLORS
342	🄰	153	Very light violet
102	⊕	154	Very dark grape
1049	↵	301	Medium mahogany
46	⊗	666	Bright red
300	T	745	Light pale yellow
275	↘	746	Off white
360	◣	898	Very dark coffee brown
187	▣	958	Dark seagreen
186	△	959	Medium seagreen
185	∷	964	Light seagreen
35	Y	3705	Dark melon
33	☆	3706	Medium melon
31	O	3708	Light melon
35	·│·	3801	Very dark melon
188	//	3812	Very dark seagreen
873	▷	3834	Dark grape
872	‡	3835	Medium grape
869	⊥	3836	Light grape
1003	✕	3853	Dark autumn gold
1002	∩	3854	Medium autumn gold
301	⊛	3855	Light autumn gold

BACKSTITCH (2X)

ANCHOR		DMC	COLORS
46	—	666	Bright red*
360	—	898	Very dark coffee brown*
188	—	3812	Very dark seagreen*

*Duplicate color

A Gift for You

A GIFT FOR YOU
CROSS-STITCH (3X)

ANCHOR		DMC	COLORS
342		153	Very light violet
102		154	Very dark grape
358		433	Medium brown
46		666	Bright red
300		745	Light pale yellow
275		746	Off white
360		898	Very dark coffee brown
187		958	Dark seagreen
186		959	Medium seagreen
185		964	Light seagreen
35		3705	Dark melon
33		3706	Medium melon
31		3708	Light melon
35		3801	Very dark melon
188		3812	Very dark seagreen
873		3834	Dark grape
872		3835	Medium grape
869		3836	Light grape
1002		3854	Medium autumn gold
301		3855	Light autumn gold

BACKSTITCH (2X)

ANCHOR		DMC	COLORS
102	—	154	Very dark grape*
360	—	898	Very dark coffee brown*
188	—	3812	Very dark seagreen*

Duplicate color

From Our Kitchen

FROM OUR KITCHEN
CROSS-STITCH (3X)

ANCHOR		DMC	COLORS
342		153	Very light violet
102		154	Very dark grape
46		666	Bright red
360		898	Very dark coffee brown
187		958	Dark seagreen
186		959	Medium seagreen
185		964	Light seagreen
292		3078	Very light golden yellow
35		3705	Dark melon
33		3706	Medium melon
31		3708	Light melon
35		3801	Very dark melon
188		3812	Very dark seagreen

CROSS-STITCH (3X)

ANCHOR		DMC	COLORS
306		3820	Dark straw
305		3821	Straw
295		3822	Light straw
873		3834	Dark grape
872		3835	Medium grape
869		3836	Light grape
307		3852	Very dark straw

BACKSTITCH (2X)

ANCHOR		DMC	COLORS
360	—	898	Very dark coffee brown*
188	—	3812	Very dark seagreen*

Duplicate color

Kitchen Sampler

Design by Lois Winston

This apron deserves to be on display all year round to show off your love of stitching.

Materials

- Antique white 28-count Lugana: 15 x 21 inches
- Bib apron of choice

"Kitchen Sampler" was stitched on antique white 28-count Lugana from Zweigart using floss from DMC.

Skill Level

**Average

Stitch Count

137 wide x 137 high

Approximate Design Size

11-count 12½" x 12½"
14-count 9¾" x 9¾"
16-count 8½" x 8½"
18-count 7⅝" x 7⅝"
22-count 6¼" x 6¼"
28-count over two threads 9¾" x 9¾"

Instructions

1. Center and stitch design on 28-count Lugana, stitching over two threads using two strands floss for Cross-Stitch and French Knot; two strands floss for Backstitch on letters, grape and strawberry tendrils; and one strand floss for all other Backstitch.

Finishing

2. Hand- or machine-stitch finished piece according to manufacturer's instructions. ❖

CROSS-STITCH (2X)

ANCHOR	DMC	COLORS
2	White	White
1006	304	Medium red
403	310	Black
399	318	Light steel grey
1025	347	Very dark salmon
401	413	Dark pewter grey
235	414	Dark steel grey
358	433	Medium brown
1046	435	Very light brown
362	437	Light tan
683	500	Very dark blue green
878	501	Dark blue green
876	503	Medium blue green
933	543	Ultra very light beige brown
926	712	Cream
387	739	Ultra very light tan
316	740	Tangerine
303	742	Light tangerine
301	744	Pale yellow
1021	761	Light salmon
234	762	Very light pearl grey
259	772	Very light yellow green
131	798	Dark delft blue
359	801	Dark coffee brown
130	809	Delft blue
45	814	Dark garnet
134	820	Very dark royal blue
378	841	Light beige brown
368	842	Very light beige brown
1044	895	Very dark hunter green
246	986	Very dark forest green
242	989	Forest green
266	3347	Medium yellow green
264	3348	Light yellow green
1023	3712	Medium salmon
868	3779	Ultra very light terra cotta
896	3858	Medium rosewood
894	3859	Light rosewood

BACKSTITCH (2X)

ANCHOR	DMC	COLORS
403	310	Black* (letters on jars; tendrils on grapes, strawberry and eggplant)
1044	895	Very dark hunter green* (letters with heart)

BACKSTITCH (1X)

ANCHOR	DMC	COLOR
403	310	Black*

FRENCH KNOT (2X)

ANCHOR	DMC	COLORS
403	310	Black*
1044	895	Very dark hunter green*

Duplicate color

Jar Lids

Design by Lois Winston

Add an extra touch to a gift of homemade goodies with these stitched jar toppers.

Materials for Each
• Jar lid cover with 3-inch Aida insert

Skill Level
*Easy

Stitch Count for Each
21 wide x 21 high

Approximate Design Size
11-count 2" x 2"
14-count 1½" x 1½"
16-count 1⅜" x 1⅜"
18-count 1¼" x 1¼"
22-count 1" x 1"

Instructions
1. Center and stitch design of choice, using three strands floss for Cross-Stitch, two strands floss for Backstitch and one strand floss for French Knot. ❖

Strawberry Jam

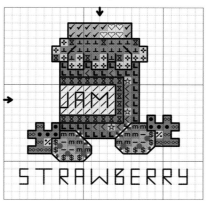

Seeds

STRAWBERRY JAM
CROSS-STITCH (3X)

ANCHOR		DMC	COLORS
218	∞	319	Very dark pistachio green
9046	☆	321	Red
59	$	326	Very dark rose
38	m	335	Rose
217	●	367	Dark pistachio green
261	⅞	368	Light pistachio green
1005	<	498	Dark red
926	/	712	Cream
890	♡	729	Medium old gold
941	X	792	Dark cornflower blue
131	⊥	798	Dark delft blue
144	✦	800	Pale delft blue
45	L	814	Dark garnet
36	–	3326	Light rose
374	✓	3829	Very dark old gold

BACKSTITCH (2X)

ANCHOR		DMC	COLORS
403	—	310	Black
941	—	792	Dark cornflower blue*

FRENCH KNOT (1X)

ANCHOR		DMC	COLOR
403	●	310	Black*

Duplicate color

SEEDS
CROSS-STITCH (3X)

ANCHOR		DMC	COLORS
11	m	350	Medium coral
293	↑	727	Very light topaz
303	⅞	742	Light tangerine
13	L	817	Very dark coral red
229	e	910	Dark emerald green
850	◼	926	Medium gray green
848	a	927	Light gray green
274	⊥	928	Very light gray green
1015	⌘	3777	Very dark terra cotta
1013	∞	3778	Light terra cotta
212	2	3818	Ultra very dark emerald green
341	#	3830	Terra cotta

BACKSTITCH (2X)

ANCHOR	DMC	COLORS
403	— 310	Black
212	— 3818	Ultra very dark emerald green*

Duplicate color

Fresh Produce

Designs by Pamela Kellogg

Mouthwatering colors and easy cross-stitches combine for delectable summer stitching!

Materials
- Dresden blue 20-count Lugana:
  14 x 15 inches (for Grove Fresh Lemons)
- Maize 20-count Lugana:
  14 x 15 inches (for Home Grown Melons)
- Lime green 20-count Lugana:
  14 x 15 inches (for Sweet Summer Plums)

"Fresh Produce" was stitched on 20-count Lugana by Zweigart using DMC floss. Finished pieces were custom framed.

Skill Level
**Average

Grove Fresh Lemons
Stitch Count
57 wide x 73 high

Approximate Design Size
11-count 5⅛" x 6⅝"

14-count 4" x 5¼"
16-count 3½" x 4½"
18-count 3⅛" x 4"
20-count over two threads 5¾" x 7⅜"
22-count 2½" x 3⅜"

Home Grown Melons
Stitch Count
58 wide x 74 high

Approximate Design Size
11-count 5¼" x 6¾"
14-count 4⅛" x 5¼"
16-count 3⅝" x 4⅝"
18-count 3¼" x 4"
20-count over two threads 5⅞" x 7⅜"
22-count 2⅝" x 3⅜"

Sweet Summer Plums Stitch Count
56 wide x 74 high

Approximate Design Size
11-count 5" x 6¾"
14-count 4" x 5¼"
16-count 3½" x 4⅝"
18-count 3" x 4"
20-count over two threads 5⅝" x 7⅜"
22-count 2½" x 3⅜"

1. Center and stitch design, stitching over two threads using four strands floss for Cross-Stitch and two strands floss for Backstitch. ❖

CROSS-STITCH (4X)

ANCHOR	DMC		COLORS
2	White		White
403	310		Black
400	317		Pewter gray
399	318		Light steel gray
218	319		Very dark pistachio green
215	320		Medium pistachio green
38	335		Rose
217	367		Dark pistachio green
261	368		Light pistachio green
1043	369		Very light pistachio green
401	413		Dark pewter gray
235	414		Dark steel gray
398	415		Pearl gray
305	725		Medium light topaz
295	726		Light topaz
293	727		Very light topaz
275	746		Off white
234	762		Very light pearl gray
259	772		Very light yellow green
24	776		Medium pink
133	796		Dark royal blue
132	797		Royal blue
131	798		Dark delft blue
136	799		Medium delft blue
130	809		Delft blue
23	818		Baby pink
271	819		Light baby pink
134	820		Very dark royal blue
218	890		Ultra dark pistachio green
1044	895		Very dark hunter green
52	899		Medium rose
292	3078		Very light golden yellow
36	3326		Light rose
268	3345		Dark hunter green
267	3346		Hunter green
266	3347		Medium yellow green
264	3348		Light yellow green
236	3799		Very dark pewter gray
275	3823		Ultra pale yellow

BACKSTITCH (2X)

ANCHOR	DMC		COLORS
2	White		White* (lemon sections)
403	310		Black* (daisy centers, lettering, plum stem)
235	414		Dark steel gray* (daisy petals)
305	725		Medium light topaz* (lemon)
134	820		Very dark royal blue* (plums)
1044	895		Very dark hunter green* (leaves, curlicue stems)

*Duplicate color

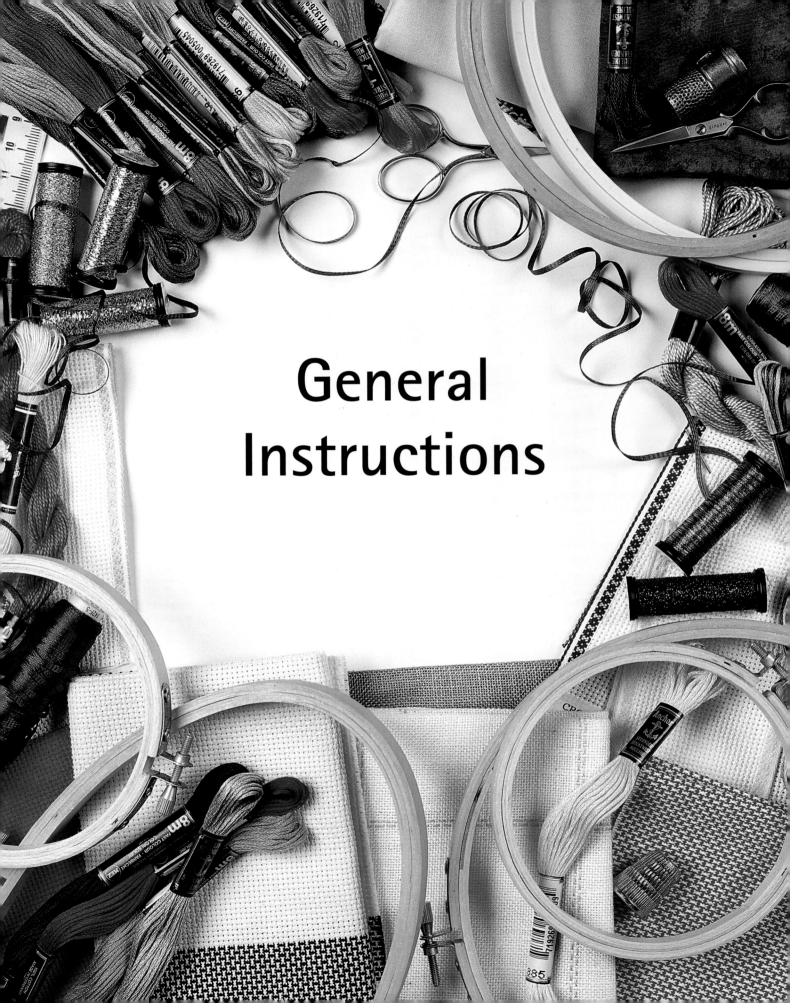

General Instructions

Tools of the Stitcher

Fabrics

Most counted cross-stitch projects are worked on evenweave fabrics made especially for counted thread embroidery. These fabrics have vertical and horizontal threads of uniform thickness and spacing. Aida cloth is a favorite of beginning stitchers because its weave forms distinctive squares in the fabric, which makes placing stitches easy.

To determine a fabric's thread count, count the number of threads per inch of fabric.

Linen is made from fibers of the flax plant and is strong and durable. Its lasting quality makes it the perfect choice for heirloom projects. Linen is available in a range of muted colors and stitch counts.

In addition to evenweave fabrics, many stitchers enjoy using waste canvas and perforated paper.

Waste canvas is basted to clothing or other fabric, forming a grid for stitching which is later removed. Perforated paper has holes evenly spaced for 14 stitches per inch.

Needles

Cross-stitch needles should have elongated eyes and blunt points. They should slip easily between the threads of the fabric, but should not pierce the fabric. The most common sizes used for cross-stitching are size 24 or 26. The ideal needle size is just small enough to slip easily through your fabric. Some stitchers prefer to use a slightly smaller needle for backstitching. When stitching on waste canvas, use a sharp needle.

Hoops, Frames & Scissors

Hoops can be round or oval and come in many sizes. The three main types are plastic, spring-tension and wooden. Frames are easier on the fabric than hoops and come in many sizes and shapes. Once fabric is mounted it doesn't have to be removed until stitching is complete, saving fabric from excessive handling.

Small, sharp scissors are essential for cutting floss and removing mistakes. For cutting fabrics, invest in a top-quality pair of medium-sized sewing scissors. To keep them in top form, use these scissors only for cutting fabrics and floss.

Stitching Threads

Today's cross-stitcher can achieve a vast array of effects in texture, color and shine. In addition to the perennial favorite, six-strand floss, stitchers can choose from sparkling metallics, shiny rayons, silks, narrow ribbon threads and much more.

Six-Strand Floss

Six-strand floss comes in a variety of colors and is available in metallics, silk and rayon as well as cotton. Most projects are worked using two or three strands of floss for cross-stitches and one or two strands for backstitches. For ease of stitching and to prevent wear on fibers, use lengths no longer than 18 inches.

Pearl Cotton

Pearl cotton is available in #3, #5, #8 and #12, with #3 being the thickest. The plies of pearl cotton will not separate, and for most stitching one strand is used. Pearl cotton has a lustrous sheen.

Flower & Ribbon Threads

Flower thread has a tight twist and comes in many soft colors. It is heavier than one ply of six-strand floss—one strand of flower thread equals two strands of floss. Ribbon thread is a narrow ribbon especially created for stitching. It comes in a large number of colors in satin as well as metallic finishes.

Blending Filament & Metallic Braid

Blending filament is a fine, shiny fiber that can be used alone or combined with floss or other thread. Knotting the blending filament on the needle with a slipknot is recommended for control.

Metallic braid is a braided metallic fiber, usually used single-ply. Thread this fiber just as you would any other fiber. Use short lengths, about 15 inches, to keep the fiber from fraying.

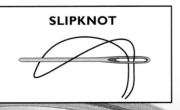

SLIPKNOT

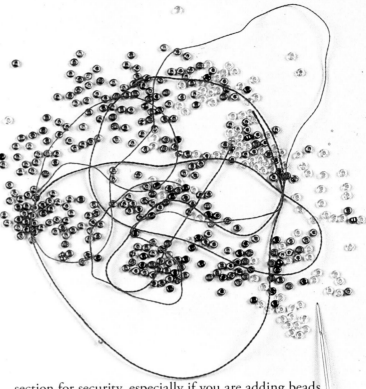

Stitching With Beads

Small seed beads can be added to any cross-stitch design, using one bead per stitch. Knot thread at beginning of beaded section for security, especially if you are adding beads to clothing. The bead should lie in the same direction as the top half of cross-stitches.

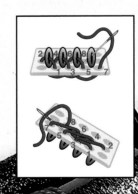

Bead Attachment

Use one strand floss to secure beads. Bring beading needle up from back of work, leaving 2 inches length of thread hanging; do not knot (end will be secured between stitches as you work). Thread bead on needle; complete stitch.

Do not skip over more than two stitches or spaces without first securing thread, or last bead will be loose. To secure, weave thread into several stitches on back of work. Follow graph to work design, using one bead per stitch.

Before You Begin

Assemble fabric, floss, pattern and tools. Familiarize yourself with the graph, color key and instructions before beginning.

Preparing Fabric

Before you stitch, decide how large to cut fabric. If you are making a pillow or other design which requires a large unstitched area, be sure to leave plenty of fabric. If you are making a small project, leave at least 3 inches around all edges of design. Determine the design area size by using this formula: number of stitches across design area divided by the number of threads per inch of fabric equals size of fabric in inches. Measure fabric, then cut evenly along horizontal and vertical threads.

Press out folds. To prevent raveling, hand overcast or machine zigzag fabric edges. Find center of fabric by folding horizontally and vertically, and mark with a small stitch.

Reading Graphs

Cross-stitch graphs or charts are made up of colors and symbols to tell you the exact color, type and placement of each stitch. Each square represents the area for one complete cross-stitch. Next to each graph, there is a key with information about stitches and floss colors represented by the graph's colors and symbols.

Some graphs are so large they must be divided for printing.

Preparing Floss

The six strands of floss are easily separated, and the number of strands used is given in instructions. Cut strands in 14–18 inches lengths. When separating floss, always separate all six strands, then recombine the number of strands needed. To make floss separating easier, run cut length across a damp sponge. To prevent floss from tangling, run cut length through a fabric-softener dryer sheet before separating and threading needle. To colorfast red floss tones, which sometimes bleed, hold floss under running water until water runs clear. Allow to air dry.

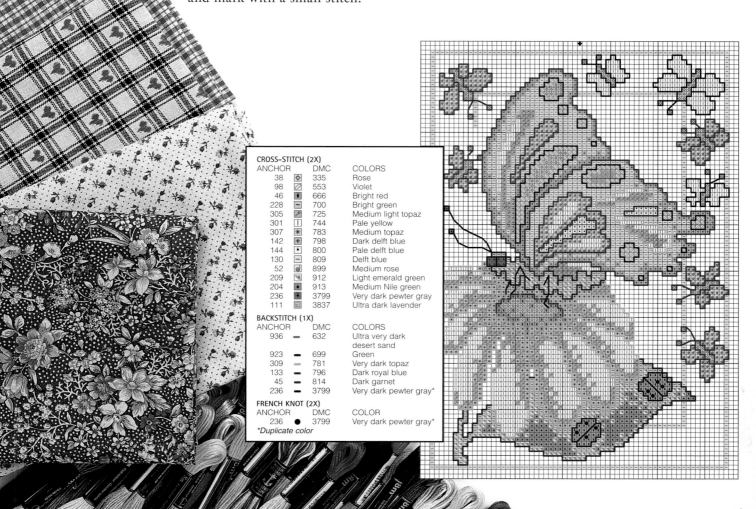

CROSS-STITCH (2X)

ANCHOR		DMC	COLORS
38		335	Rose
98		553	Violet
46		666	Bright red
228		700	Bright green
305		725	Medium light topaz
301		744	Pale yellow
307		783	Medium topaz
142		798	Dark delft blue
144		800	Pale delft blue
130		809	Delft blue
52		899	Medium rose
209		912	Light emerald green
204		913	Medium Nile green
236		3799	Very dark pewter gray
111		3837	Ultra dark lavender

BACKSTITCH (1X)

ANCHOR		DMC	COLORS
936	—	632	Ultra very dark desert sand
923	—	699	Green
309	—	781	Very dark topaz
133	—	796	Dark royal blue
45	—	814	Dark garnet
236	—	3799	Very dark pewter gray*

FRENCH KNOT (2X)

ANCHOR		DMC	COLOR
236	●	3799	Very dark pewter gray*

*Duplicate color

Stitching Techniques

Beginning & Ending a Thread

Try these methods for beginning a thread, then decide which one is best for you.

Securing the thread: Start by pulling needle through fabric back to front, leaving about 1 inch behind fabric. Hold this end with fingers as you begin stitching, and work over end with your first few stitches. After work is in progress, weave end through the back of a few stitches.

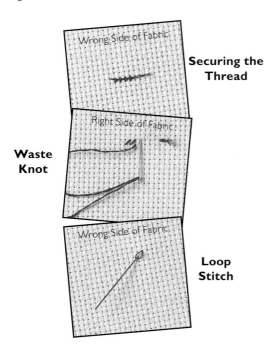

Securing the Thread

Waste Knot

Loop Stitch

Waste knot: Make a knot in end of floss and pull needle through fabric front to back several squares over from where your first cross-stitch will be. Come up at first stitch and stitch first few stitches over floss end. Clip knot.

Loop stitch: This method can only be used for even numbers of strands. Cut strands twice the normal length, then take half the number of strands needed and fold in half. Insert loose ends in needle and bring needle up from back at first stitch, leaving loop underneath. Take needle down through fabric and through loop; pull to secure.

For even stitches, keep a consistent tension on your thread, and pull thread and needle completely through fabric with each stab of the needle. Make all the top crosses on your cross-stitches face the same direction. To finish a

thread, run the needle under the back side of several stitches and clip. Threads carried across the back of unworked areas may show through to the front, so do not carry threads.

Master Stitchery

Work will be neater if you always try to make each stitch by coming up in an unoccupied hole and going down in an occupied hole.

The sewing method is preferred for stitching on linen and some other evenweaves, but can also be used on Aida. Stitches are made as in hand-sewing with needle going from front to back to front of fabric in one motion. All work is done from the front of the fabric. When stitching with the sewing method, it is important not to pull thread too tightly or stitches will become distorted. Stitching on linen is prettiest with the sewing method, using no hoop. If you use a hoop or frame when using the

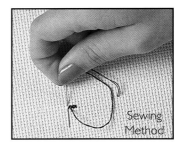

Sewing Method

sewing method with Aida, keep in mind that fabric cannot be pulled taut. There must be "give" in the fabric in order for needle to slip in and out easily.

In the stab method, needle and floss are taken completely through fabric twice with each stitch. For the first half of the stitch, bring needle up and pull thread completely through fabric to the front. Then take needle down and reach underneath and pull completely through to bottom.

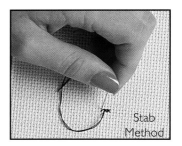

Stab Method

Working on Evenweave

When working on linen or other evenweave fabric, keep needle on right side of fabric, taking needle front to back to front with each stitch.

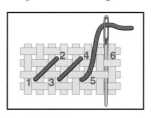

Work over two threads, placing the beginning and end of the bottom half of the first cross-stitch where a vertical thread crosses a horizontal thread.

Cleaning Your Needlework

Careful washing, pressing and sometimes blocking help preserve and protect your stitched piece. After stitching is complete, a gentle washing will remove surface dirt, hoop marks and hand oils that have accumulated on your fabric while stitching. Even if a piece looks clean, it's always a good idea to give it a nice cleaning before finishing. Never press your work before cleaning, as this only serves to set those hoop marks and soils that are best removed.

Using a gentle soap such as baby shampoo or gentle white dishwashing liquid and a large, clean bowl, make a solution of cool, sudsy water. If you use a hand-wash product, make sure the one you choose contains no chlorine bleach. Fill another bowl or sink with plain cool water for rinsing.

Soak your stitched piece in sudsy water for five to ten minutes. Then gently and without rubbing or twisting, squeeze suds through fabric several times. Dip piece several times in fresh, cool water, until no suds remain.

On rare occasions floss colors will run or fade slightly. When this happens, continue to rinse in cool water until water becomes perfectly clear. Remove fabric from water and lay on a soft, white towel. Never twist or wring your work. Blot excess water away and roll the piece up in the towel, pressing gently.

Never allow a freshly washed piece of embroidery to air dry. Instead, remove the damp piece from the towel and place face down on a fresh, dry white towel. To prevent color stains, it's important to keep the stitched piece flat, not allowing stitched areas to touch each other or other areas of the fabric. Make sure the edges of fabric are in straight lines and even. To be sure fabric edges are straight when pressing dry, use a ruler or T-square to check edges. Wash towel several times before using it to block cross-stitch, and use it only for this purpose.

After edges are aligned and fabric is perfectly smooth, cover the back of the stitched piece with a pressing cloth, cotton diaper or other lightweight white cotton cloth. Press dry with a dry iron set on a high permanent press or cotton setting, depending on fabric content. Allow stitchery to lie in this position several hours. Machine-drying is acceptable after use for items like towels and kitchen accessories, but your work will be prettier and smoother if you give these items a careful pressing the first time.

Framing and Mounting

Shopping for Frames

When you shop for a frame, take the stitchery along with you and compare several frame and mat styles. Keep in mind the "feeling" of your stitched piece when choosing a frame. For example, an exquisite damask piece stitched with metallics and silk threads might need an ornate gold frame, while a primitive sampler stitched on dirty linen with flower thread would need a simpler, perhaps wooden frame.

Mounting

Cross-stitch pieces can be mounted on mat board, white cardboard, special padded or unpadded mounting boards designed specifically for needle-work, or special acid-free mat board available from art-supply stores. Acid-free framing materials are the best choice for projects you wish to keep well-preserved for future generations. If you prefer a padded look, cut quilt batting to fit mounting board.

Center blocked stitchery over mounting board of choice with quilt batting between, if desired. Leaving 1½ to 3 inches around all edges, trim excess fabric away along straight of grain.

Mounting boards made for needlework have self-stick surfaces and require no pins. When using these products, lift and smooth needlework onto board until work is taut and edges are smooth and even. Turn board face down and smooth fabric to back, mitering corners.

Pins are required for other mounting boards. With design face up, keeping fabric straight and taut, insert a pin through fabric and edge of mounting board at the center of each side. Turn piece face down and smooth excess fabric to back, mitering corners.

There are several methods for securing fabric edges. Edges may be glued to mat board with liquid fabric glue or fabric glue stick. If mat board is thick, fabric may be stapled.

Mats & Glass

Precut mats are available in many sizes and colors to fit standard-size frames. Custom mats are available in an even wider variety of colors, textures and materials. Using glass over cross-stitch is a matter of personal preference, but is generally discouraged. Moisture can collect behind glass and rest on fabric, causing mildew stains. A single or double mat will hold glass away from fabric.

Stitch Guide

Basic Stitchery

Cross-Stitch: There are two ways of making a basic Cross-Stitch. The first method is used when working rows of stitches in the same color. The first step makes the bottom half of the stitches across the row, and the second step makes the top half.

The second method is used when making single stitches. The bottom and top halves of each stitch are worked before starting the next stitch.

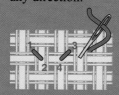
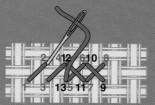
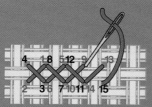

Quarter Cross-Stitch: Stitch may slant in any direction.

Three-Quarter Cross-Stitch A Half Cross-Stitch plus a Quarter Cross-Stitch may slant in any direction.

Half Cross-Stitch: The first part of a Cross-Stitch may slant in either direction.

Embellishing With Embroidery

EMBROIDERY stitches add detail and dimension to stitching. Unless otherwise noted, work Backstitches first, then other embroidery stitches.

Backstitch (B'st)

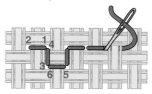

French Knot (Fr)

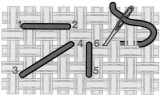

Straight Stitch (Str)

Special Stitches

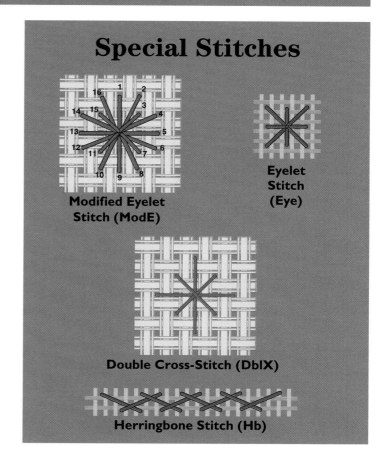

Modified Eyelet Stitch (ModE)

Eyelet Stitch (Eye)

Double Cross-Stitch (DblX)

Herringbone Stitch (Hb)

Cross-Stitch Supplies

Page 6: *Watering Cans*

- Jonquil yellow 14-count Aida by Wichelt Imports Inc.

- Shaker Peg Rack #10101 by Sudberry House

Page 15: *Dragonflies*

- Delicate teal 28-count Jobelan by Wichelt Imports Inc.

Page 18: *Garden Buddies*

- White 14-count Aida by Zweigart

- Seed beads by Mill Hill

- Black 26-gauge wire by Artistic Wire

Page 20: *Bumblebee Fancy*

- Opalescent 14-count Aida by Zweigart

- 4-inch Nantucket Basket #30000 with 4-inch Pincushion Insert #30001 by Sudberry House

- #8 fine braid by Kreinik Mfg. Co. Inc.

Page 21: *Classic Flowers*

- White 28-count Meran by Zweigart

- Antique Finish 8-inch bell pull #201420 by Wichelt Imports Inc.

Page 24: *Mexican Talavera Tile*

- Antique white 14-count Lady Elizabeth pillow sham #PS7780-0322 by Charles Craft Inc.

Page 25: *Chapeau Rouge*

- Angel Blush 28-count Lugana by Zweigart

- Blending filament and #4 very fine braid by Kreinik Mfg. Co. Inc.

- Glass seed beads by Mill Hill

Page 28: *With All My Heart*

- Ivory 28-count Jobelan by Wichelt Imports Inc.

Page 32: *Miniature Roses*

- Antique white 28-count Jobelan by Wichelt Imports Inc.

Page 33: *Water Bird*

- Natural 14-count Aida by Charles Craft Inc.

Page 35: *Oriental Poppy Beverage Set*

- Black classic reserve 14-count Aida by Charles Craft Inc.

- Black lacquer tray #65647 and coasters #95037 by Sudberry House

Page 38: *Rose Heart*

- White 25-count Lugana by Wichelt Imports Inc.

Page 39: *Butterfly Table Topper*

- Ivory 20-count linen Austria table topper #14037/02 by Brunner Haus

- Silk Mori threads by Kreinik Mfg. Co. Inc.

- Glass beads by Mill Hill

Page 49: *Bloomin' Blazes*

- White 20-count Lugana by Zweigart

Page 52: *Blue Bells*

- White 22-count Vienna by Wichelt Imports Inc.

Page 58: *Sunflowers*

- Forget-me-not blue 28-count linen by Wichelt Imports Inc.

- Blending filament by Kreinik Mfg. Co. Inc.

Page 60: *Antique House Sampler*

- Café mocha 32-count country French linen by Wichelt Imports Inc.

- Sampler threads by The Gentle Art

Page 67: *Garden Friends Sampler*

- Antique white 28-count Jobelan by Wichelt Imports Inc.

- Bumblebees #86128 and marten house #86130 buttons by Mill Hill

Page 70: *Happiest Heart Sampler*

- White 14-count Aida by Zweigart

Page 74: *Roses & Thorns*

- Light rose 14-count Aida by Zweigart

- Mirror frame #MAH1572 by Olde Colonial Designs

Page 75: *Misty Lavender Sampler*

- Antique white 28-count Alma cloth by Wichelt Imports Inc.

- Frosted and glass seed beads by Mill Hill

- Silk Mori floss, Silk Serica floss, #8 fine braid, #4 very fine braid and tapestry braid by Kreinik Mfg. Co. Inc.

Page 78: *Happiness & Simplicity Mini Samplers*

- White 18-count Aida by Zweigart

Page 81: *Bold Blooms*

- Antique white 28-count Jobelan by Wichelt Imports Inc.

Page 88: *Garden Creatures*

- White 14-count Aida by Wichelt Imports Inc.

Page 93: *Lo, the Winter Is Over*

- Antique white 32-count Belfast linen by Zweigart

Page 96: *Heart's Delight Pillow*

- White 32-count Lugana by Zweigart

Page 98: *Love Is a Gift*

- Bridal white 30-count Melinda by Wichelt Imports Inc.

Page 101: *My Daughter, My Treasure*

- Cream 32-count pure Irish linen by Charles Craft Inc.

- Seed beads and small bugle beads by Mill Hill

- Square box #99001 wood stain by Sudberry House

Page 103: *Floral Teacup*

- Daffodil 20-count Laguna by Zweigart

Page 105: *Patchwork Welcome*

- Antique white 14-count Aida by Wichelt Imports Inc.

Page 108: *If Friends Were Flowers*

- Daffodil 22-count Softana by Zweigart

- Crystal seed beads #00161 by Mill Hill

Page 110: *Country Sentiments Dish Towels*

- Ecru 14-count showcase huck towel HF-6500-6750 by Charles Craft Inc.

Page 116: *Russian Khokhloma—Berries*

- Light sand 28-count Cashel linen by Zweigart

- Small collector's cabinet #35341 by Sudberry House

Page 118: *Patchwork Pumpkin Pin*

- Antique brown 14-count perforated paper, beads and buttons by Mill Hill

Page 119: *Kitchen Alphabet*

- Antique white 28-count Lugana by Zweigart

Page 122: *Canning-Jag Tags*

- Red, brown and purple 24-gauge craft wire by American Art Clay Co. Inc. (AMACO)

Page 125: *Kitchen Sampler*

- Antique white 28-count Lugana by Zweigart

Page 130: *Fresh Produce*

- Dresden blue, maize and lime green 20-count Lugana by Zweigart

Cross-Stitch Sources

The following companies provided fabric and/or supplies for projects in this book. If you are unable to locate a product locally, contact the manufacturers listed below for the closest retail or mail-order source in your area.

American Art Clay Co. Inc.
(317) 244-6871
www.amaco.com

Artistic Wire
(630) 530-7567
www.artisticwire.com

Brunner Haus
(800) 436-8313

Charles Craft Inc.
(800) 277-0980
www.charlescraft.com

Daniel Enterprises
(800) 277-6850
www.crafterspride.com

Mill Hill
www.millhillbeads.com

Kreinik Mfg. Co. Inc.
(410) 281-0040
www.kreinik.com

Olde Colonial Designs
(781) 834-8836

Sudberry House
(860) 739-6951
www.sudberry.com

The Gentle Art
(614) 855-8346
www.thegentleart.com

Wichelt Imports Inc.
(800) 356-9516
www.wichelt.com

Zweigart
(732) 562-8888
www.zweigart.com

Special Thanks

We would like to thank the talented cross-stitch designers whose work is featured in this collection.

Carla Acosta
Antique House Sampler, 60
Happiest Heart Sampler, 70

Catherine Bussi
Happiness & Simplicity Mini Samplers, 78
Psalm 63:7, 64

Gail Bussi
Heart's Delight Pillow, 96
Lo, the Winter Is Over, 93

Polly Carbonari
Hearts & Flowers, 55

Laura Kramer Doyle
Sweetheart Roses, 42

June Fiechter
Floral Teacup, 103

Janelle Giese
Garden Friends Sampler, 67
Misty Lavender Sampler, 75

Christine Hendricks
Garden Creatures, 88

Kathleen Hurley
Blue Bells, 52

Pamela Kellogg
Butterfly Table Topper, 39

Canning-Jar Tags, 122
Chapeau Rouge, 25
Fresh Produce, 130
Sunflowers, 58
With All My Heart, 28

Robin Kingsley
Country Sentiments Dish Towels, 110
If Friends Were Flowers, 108

Janice Lockhart
My Daughter, My Treasure, 101

Julia Lucas
Roses & Thorns, 74

Patricia Martin
My First Bible, 92

Ursula Michaels
Garden Buddies, 18
Love Is a Gift, 98

Mill Hill
Patchwork Pumpkin Pin, 118

Hope Murphy
Oriental Poppy Beverage Set, 35

Roberta Rankin
Garden Angel, 113
Rose Heart, 38

Annette Rogers
Bloomin' Blazes, 49

Barbara Sestok
Mexican Talavera Tile, 24
Russian Khokhloma—Berries, 116

Dayna Stedry
Flower Boxes, 46

True Colors
Bright Butterflies, 12
Butterflies Are Free, 9

Mike Vickery
Bumblebee Fancy, 20
Classic Flowers, 21
Dragonflies, 15
Water Bird, 33
Watering Cans, 6

Lois Winston
Jar Lids, 128
Kitchen Alphabet, 119
Kitchen Sampler, 125
Miniature Roses, 32
Patchwork Welcome, 105

Kathy Wirth
Bold Blooms, 81